A Holy Curiosity

A Holy Curiosity:

STORIES OF A LIBERAL RELIGIOUS FAITH

Bruce T. Marshall

Unitarian Universalist Fellowship
of Huntington

Edited by Mary Jane Curry
Designed by Suzanne Morgan

The personal stories in this book are reprinted with the permission of the authors.

Unitarian Universalist Fellowship of Huntington
109 Brown's Road
Huntington, New York 11743

ISBN 0-9626716-0-6

AT

Contents

Never lose a holy curiosity.

—*Albert Einstein*

Introduction

I once was at the podiatrist's having my feet examined. While the doctor checked one foot and then the other, he told me about his life. As a boy, this man had trouble with his feet and suffered much pain. That ordeal piqued his interest in podiatry and led him to devote his life to curing feet.

In that encounter I may have happened upon a truth of the human condition, for my troubles have also led into my profession. With me the issue has not been feet. Rather, I am pursued by a set of questions. Who am I? What do I trust? In what do I find meaning? How do I understand death? Who or what is God? What brings me hope? From my struggles with these questions of human existence has come my calling: the Unitarian Universalist ministry.

This experience shatters an assumption I used to make of how people choose their life's work. I had thought that people make a career of what they do best. Those good at tinkering become mechanics. The best students become teachers. The people with the most perfect feet become podiatrists. Those with answers to life's questions enter the clergy.

But I had trouble answering life's questions, and I still do. Amidst all the roles I play in life and the demands I try to meet, I wonder: Who am I? Who do I seek to be? I sort through the experiences of my life and the information and the opinions to which I am subjected daily, and I wonder what I can trust to help me make sense of it. I listen to people speak of God and the attributes they give to this Being, and I wonder if there is a God I can experience. I think about death and how it changes everything, and I wonder how I should live, knowing that

I will die. I meet difficult times in my days and in those of people close to me—times of struggle and suffering—and I look for that which may sustain us. Where do we find courage to face life's terrors, and to seek its possibilities?

These concerns keep at me. I may not have final answers, but I do have considerable experience dealing with questions. My ministry—and this book—is based on the encounter with the questions of existence.

Religion is concerned with ultimate questions. Each faith offers responses to humankind's wondering about the meanings and possibilities of being. Doctrinal statements, parables, services of worship, and sacred texts all address the underlying questions of existence.

Religious congregations—whether churches, synagogues, fellowships, mosques or temples—provide contexts in which people can examine ultimate questions. A Roman Catholic church provides different guidance than a Buddhist temple. A Jewish synagogue offers a different set of practices and experiences than a Native American community. But each—no matter how varied the beliefs and customs—enables participants to engage the ultimate questions of existence.

For my own seeking, I have chosen the context of the liberal religious tradition as expressed in Unitarian Universalist congregations. In a sense, this was an easy choice, since I was raised as a Unitarian Universalist, and liberal religious values are part of my being. But I continue to be enriched and given valuable counsel as I share my journey with other religious liberals. Within this community of shared values, I am best able to pursue the questions of existence.

The Unitarian Universalist tradition stretches back in history. On the North American continent, Unitarian and Universalist beginnings are found in the eighteenth century as some New England congregations sought a faith more human and humane than the dominant Puritan orthodoxy. The tradition stretches back to a vision of a rational and socially concerned faith articulated in seventeenth-century England and to a faith of tolerance and openness in Eastern Europe in the sixteenth century. This history connects me with people through the years who questioned religious dogma and sought the freedom to seek their own ways to respond to life's questions.

Today's Unitarian Universalist congregations, inheritors of a rich history of religious reform, are a diverse group. They are joined, however, by certain practices and common values, including:

(1) a non-dogmatic approach to religious questions. This commit-
    ment to freedom of religion is reflected in the lack of a creed in
    Unitarian Universalist congregations.
(2) a history that emerged from Christianity but whose stance of
    tolerance and openness to difference has led many people of
    Jewish and non-Western religious backgrounds to find a religious
    home in the Unitarian Universalist community.
(3) an insistence upon human dignity and the inherent worth of each
    person.
(4) a commitment to the ongoing search for truth and meaning as
    essential to the religious enterprise. Religious teachings, we be-
    lieve, must be subject to the tests of reason and experience.
(5) respect for the voice of conscience when we face the hard choices
    of life. Our approach is to nourish ethical sensibility and respon-
    sibility rather than to impose rules.
(6) congregations based in the free choice of participants to join
    together and create a religious community.

Congregations guided by such affirmations and practices offer a
distinctive range of responses to the questions of existence. To be
sure, the attitude of openness in the liberal religious tradition makes
us resist final answers. We believe that revelation is continuous, not
a one-time phenomenon, and that it is supplemented by ongoing
investigation and discussion. This openness leads some people to
charge that we have no answers at all. I disagree completely with that
assessment, for within Unitarian Universalism I find powerful guidance as I ponder the questions of my life.

My purpose in writing, then, is to reflect upon religious questions
and suggest responses that I find contained within the liberal religious
vision. I don't claim to speak for all Unitarian Universalists, and I
don't expect everyone to agree with my conclusions. I offer my
personal response to the questions of existence, a response guided
by my interaction with the values and people of liberal religious
congregations.

I draw upon several sources for these responses: the values and affirmations of our tradition, examples from the history of religious liberalism, reflections by other Unitarian Universalists. But my primary

sources are real stories and experiences that articulate the faith of Unitarian Universalists.

Storytelling is a universal human characteristic that helps us make sense of our lives. It gives form, meaning, and direction to the events of our days. As the Roman Catholic theologian John Shea expresses it in *Stories of God*,

> No matter our mood, in reverie or expectation, panic or peace, we can be found stringing together incidents, and unfolding episodes. We turn our pain into narrative so we can bear it; we turn our ecstasy into narrative so we can prolong it. We all seem to be under the sentence of Scheherazade. We tell our stories to live.

Religions are introduced and explained and spread through stories: the parables of Jesus, the stories of the Talmud, the Buddha, the Hindu gods, and the tales of the Native American religions. These stories tell the central concepts of a faith and its responses to our questions.

Stories also show how we experience religious affirmation in everyday life. Even if it is possible to articulate a religion's beliefs clearly, its real test comes when its principles are applied to living. Do they help us become better people? Are we empowered to face the problems and the possibilities of life?

This book draws upon stories and experiences Unitarian Universalists tell about their faith. Some were responses to requests I made in Unitarian Universalist publications for people to write accounts of what has made a difference in their lives. Some were written in workshops that I conducted. Some have been shared in worship services, and some I came across in books or articles by Unitarian Universalists. Some of these stories are my own.

These stories include responses to the questions—of identity and meaning and truth and hope—that underlie our everyday experience. There are occasions when people made a decision or took a stand or realized something important about who they wanted to be. In these stories, our principles are given flesh.

I feel privileged to share my life with the people of Unitarian Universalist congregations. They inspire me, challenge me, urge me to think in new ways. They also have shown me considerable caring and love. I like Unitarian Universalists and consider their presence in my life a gift.

This brings me to my final purpose: to promote Unitarian Universalist congregations as places where people can engage the questions of life within a caring community. If you are a Unitarian Universalist, I hope these reflections will deepen your appreciation of our faith, and that you will be encouraged to consider the questions of your life. If you are seeking a religious home, I hope this book will prompt you to consider a Unitarian Universalist congregation.

I want to express my thanks to the congregation I serve, The Unitarian Universalist Fellowship of Huntington, New York, for the support I have received throughout this project. I want to thank my wife, Patricia Creatura, for her encouragement and her patience. And I want to thank the many Unitarian Universalists who have enriched my days and given me courage to explore the ultimate questions of life.

Bruce T. Marshall

CHAPTER 1

WHO AM I?

What can I expect of myself? Who may I become? These questions are personal, but they also are religious. They address not simply the issue of one's own nature but also that of the human species. What is our place in the world? Who are we called to be?

I was sent to a religious school at the age of thirteen because my parents believed I was a bad girl. I had ditched class at the local junior high because the teacher was ridiculing me in front of the class. I was the only Mexican in school. Though the class had voted me secretary, the teacher took every opportunity to be sarcastic when I did anything. To save face I ditched class; my parents were horrified at my spunk and to a private school I was sent.

When the instructors severely punished my classmates for their unruliness, I became good. I followed and did as I was told. I continued to obey in marriage and had six children. One day I went out of my mind believing I was pregnant again. This forced me to decide I was taking responsibility for my own life, my body, and own punishment.

I decided to formulate my own beliefs based on my experience. The road was rough. I had pangs of doubt and fear. Somehow, I was introduced to the Unitarian Universalists at the Pacific Unitarian Church in Southern California. They initiated programs and acted out of their own concerns freely. Never had I experienced such openness.

I could not believe the Unitarian Universalists' freedom to express themselves. Their influence, the environment, helped me venture forth to take responsibility by allowing me to express opinions, take part in social concerns and make an impact to make this a better world. I feel alive again part of this community of Unitarian Universalists.

Lydia Flores
Pacific Unitarian Church
Palos Verdes, California

Who am I? The question springs from the center of each person's being.

American Unitarianism and Universalism began in an eighteenth-century dispute with religious orthodoxy. A key issue concerned this question: Who am I? What can I expect of myself and of the men and the women with whom I share this earth?

The orthodox held that human beings are inherently sinful. As the Old Testament tells it, Adam and Eve disobeyed God and ate from the Tree of Knowledge of Good and Evil. As punishment, they were driven from the Garden. Thus human history began. From then on, orthodoxy claims, children have come into this world bearing the sin of that first man and woman. This story expresses the human condition: we assert our wills over that of God and thereby disobey His law. Hence our sinfulness, our "utter depravity," as the orthodox preachers called it.

The liberal side, represented by the Unitarians and the Universalists, took issue with the assessment of utter depravity. They argued that the orthodox did not take seriously the human capacity for good. They also could not believe that a benevolent God would bring into the world children who must be considered sinful from the start. The liberals asserted that all human beings have the potential for both good and evil. Hence, our calling in this world is to nourish our capacity for good. The Unitarians and the Universalists looked at the human condition and found not inherent sinfulness, but inherent dignity and worth.

This dispute between religious orthodoxy and liberalism in the late eighteenth century and early nineteenth century may seem remote from today's concerns, but the issues remain with us. There still is disagreement on how to perceive the human condition, how to respond to the question, "Who am I as a human being?"

Today's orthodox continue to assert that people are fallen, sinful creatures, who require redemption. Babies are baptized, symbolizing the need to wash them clean from original sin. Orthodox congregations admit their unworthiness as part of the normal order of worship. The faithful pray for salvation to release them from this world of pain and suffering.

From many other sources comes the message that the individual is of little worth. We live in a mass society in which people often feel lost, with little power over their lives. We live in a world of much poverty, in which the shifting sands of political fate determine people's fortunes. In our society many people are cut off from communities of caring and support. Much in our everyday existence conveys a message of unworthiness and insignificance. When we ask: Who am I as a human being? the response we often hear is: A creature who scarcely matters.

In response to such slighting and demeaning, we need another way to view the human condition. Such a need existed almost 200 years ago when religious liberals set forth their vision of the human place in this world. Today there is still a need for an alternative message of human dignity and worth.

In the story that begins this chapter, Ms. Flores describes growing up with a perception of herself as "bad." As a "bad" person, her lot was to obey those in authority: her teachers, her husband, the church. She obeyed until it became clear that she was destroying herself. And so in an act of courage and strength, she determined to take responsibility for her own life. Her support in this difficult journey came from a Unitarian Universalist society. Here she found a community of people gathered around the affirmation of human dignity and human worth. Here she could feel alive again.

❖ ❖ ❖

William Ellery Channing (1780-1842) was a Boston minister and the most important leader in the early development of American Unitarianism. His words and example provided a beacon that guided our religious movement in its formative years.

As a boy, Channing was shy and sickly. He was born into a prominent family, but his father died while Channing was a teenager, leaving the family in poverty. He was often lonely; he wrestled with self-doubt; he sought to overcome his own sense of sinfulness by repudiating all pleasure. He fasted and punished himself; he sought to drive out the demons that he felt existed within himself.[1]

In the midst of such struggles while he was a student at Harvard, Channing had an experience that changed him and brought him to view life from a new perspective. His nephew, William Henry Channing, wrote,

> He was, at the time, walking as he read, beneath a clump of willows yet standing in the meadow....There burst upon his mind that view of the dignity of human nature which was ever after to uphold and cherish him....The place and hour were always sacred in his memory, and he frequently referred to them with grateful awe. It seemed to him that he then passed through a new spiritual birth, and entered upon the day of eternal peace and joy.[2]

The affirmation of human dignity was a radical message in Channing's day. It remains with us today as a central affirmation of Unitarian Universalism, and the experience of human dignity continues to be crucial in the spiritual development of religious liberals.

I remember a day when I was in the sixth grade. There was a boy who was two or three years older than he should have been as a sixth grader. He was a foot taller than any of us. His voice had already changed and was quite low, which emphasized the seriousness of his presence. He hung around with kids you would not want to come across in a dark street or a dark alley or a dark anywhere.

His name was Donald, never Don, and he was having trouble in class with an assignment. This was a read-aloud assignment so everybody was hearing him having trouble, and the teacher was prodding him. Suddenly, he stood up, said something about how he just couldn't do it, and walked out of the room.

That was unheard-of behavior in a sixth-grade class in the fifties. It was breaking a rule. You simply did not just get up and walk out of the room. And so our teacher—a man—took off in pursuit. The rest of the class sat wondering what kind of trouble Donald was going to be in now. (It didn't occur to us that the teacher may have taken a risk by chasing Donald.)

A few minutes later our teacher came back into the room with his arm around Donald: not coercively, but reassuringly. The teacher was quietly talking to him as they entered, but I couldn't hear what he was saying. Donald returned to his seat in class, and we went on to other things.

I doubt that either Donald or the teacher remembers the incident today. But I remember it as valuing a person who may not have seemed among the most valuable of human beings. I remember it as demonstrating respect for a person, even though he had broken a rule.

It is a challenge to live with respect for the worth and dignity of another. It is a gift when another treats us as deserving of respect. When we live with respect for another and when we are treated as worthy of respect, we become alive. We see ourselves in new ways.

It has taken me a good part of my life to arrive at a point where I don't feel guilty in feeling pride in my work and in myself—and mad as hell at being underpaid (as compared to a male) for some darned good work! So I guess I could say that I am a woman who has dignity, the right kind of pride, and a better feeling of self-confidence than I ever had before. I like that.

Helen Crane
Unitarian Society
New Brunswick, New Jersey

Who am I? I am a person of worth. I am a person who has the power to change in response to the challenges of life: the losses, the pain, the times of uncertainty and fear of what may lie ahead. I am not a person who gives up.

I'm not sure who I am as yet, since I'm still in the process of self-examination and reevaluation. Why so late in life? My husband died five years ago, ending a relationship that had lasted for good *and* for ill for forty years. It took me at least a year to surface from a morass of grief, anger, relief, fear, and guilt. Compounding the difficulties was a recent retirement that allowed me no surcease in busyness. My first step beyond that year was a commitment to as much honesty as I could muster, the acceptance of failed dreams and very real inadequacies as well as a limited future.

The second, more difficult step was an assessment of my strengths that included fortitude and caring. The third step was to assess my needs and respond to them. I needed friends. I needed work. I needed fun. I needed discipline. I needed praise and most of all I needed something in which I could really believe. I found a partial answer to all of that in Unitarian Universalism.

I'm by no means a finished product, however. I hope the process continues.

Elizabeth Trembicki
North Shore Unitarian Universalist Society
Plandome, New York

Who am I? I am a person of worth who is not perfect, a person with concerns and sorrows and doubts. I am a person who struggles with the issues of my life as I seek to live with integrity and affirmation and hope. I am a person who is not yet finished.

I stumbled upon Unitarian Universalism when I took a secretarial position at a Unitarian fellowship. To my happy surprise, I found a community of people committed to this life rather than a life hereafter. Within that commitment I observed an honest regard for self and for the other person. There seemed to be no duality in the lives of Unitarians. No "ought to's" that made living a daily round of guilt trips in the name of perfection. No perfection. And a lot of stumbling.

I had been moving single-mindedly all my life, I thought, toward union with the Absolute, which in Catholic theology is God, "He in Whom we live and breathe and have our being." Unitarian "being" I observed, was "is-ness," a very Zen-like quality which I found easy to accept because it was rooted in spontaneity. It unblocked the passageway to growth, the free expression of our humanness, the acceptance of individual differences within a strong bond of love.

My short journey within Unitarian Universalism has strengthened my hold on life, has led me toward the development of a credo I can live by without relinquishing values I regard as essential to right living.

Julie Eichenberger
Unitarian Universalist Fellowship
Huntington, New York

It is a simple affirmation: the dignity and worth of our sister and brother human beings, our own dignity and worth. But it has power to transform. People come into Unitarian Universalist congregations seeking the change this power can bring. It may be a person going through a divorce who looks for assurance that he or she is of worth, despite feelings of failure and loss. It may be a person who finds he or she is not easily accepted in society—a handicapped person, one who is gay or lesbian, a single person, a person of a racial minority—this individual seeks a congregation where he or she can be accepted and valued as a human being. It may be an individual facing a personal crisis who comes for support in rebuilding a sense of human dignity.

The story of recognizing human worth and dignity is old, yet experienced again by each generation—as it was experienced as new and transforming when Channing walked and read by the Charles River as a student. I do not claim that we always live by its truth, because we don't. We often fail. But the affirmation of human dignity and worth remains at the heart of the Unitarian Universalist vision.

❖ ❖ ❖

The hopes expressed in our liberal religious tradition have frequently been betrayed. People can show callous disregard and cruelty toward each other. I cannot deny the inhumanity that human beings perpetrate against each other.

But I can respond. As a human being, as a religious person, I have the power to respond when other human beings are abused. When human life is devalued, I must witness to the worth and dignity of human beings even if all I can do is say, "No. This *shall not be.*"

When people destroy themselves through self-hate, alcoholism, drugs, fear, and guilt, then we must protest. People are too valuable to allow them such a fate. And we can protest when young people are pushed aside and ignored, or when the elderly are denied a place in society that brings them dignity and respect, or when minorities are exploited.

And we can resist the fanatic who asserts that one cannot be acceptable unless one submits to the fanatic's view of the world. We can resist those who would deny the truth of any experience that does not fit within their doctrine. We can resist those who would deprive people of the opportunity to make their own choices, even if those are different from what authority sanctions.

We can protest against those who would divide the peoples of the world, who would keep blacks apart from whites, Americans from Soviets, Israelis apart from Arabs, believers from non-believers. And those who, in the spaces between these people, would breed suspicion, fear, and hatred.

We of the Unitarian Universalist tradition seek to offer an alternative to that which demeans humankind. We seek to create religious organizations that witness to human dignity and worth, as we individual Unitarian Universalists try to live with respect for each other and for ourselves.

Yes, as human beings, we are imperfect. We each have our problems. Yet each of us also has worth. The challenge is to live that affirmation. To say no when human dignity is denied so that we can speak a larger Yes to each other, to ourselves, to life.

Dag Hammarskjold wrote,

> I don't know Who—or what—put the question. I don't know when it was put. I don't even remember answering. But at some moment I did answer *Yes* to Someone—or Something—and from that hour I was certain that existence is meaningful.[3]

❖ ❖ ❖

Who am I? I am a person of dignity and worth. I share this world with other human beings of dignity and worth. Therefore, I try to live with respect for my neighbor and for myself.

I am a flawed person. I am not perfectible. But I can change. I can learn to take responsibility for my life. I can become better able to witness to the worth of human beings. I can become more compassionate, more involved in life. I can learn to recognize when people are demeaned, and I can gain courage to speak out in protest.

Through my decisions and my actions, I can make a difference in this world.

This is a simple affirmation of inherent human worth and dignity. It is not a complicated message. But it can be transforming. It can change lives.

Notes

1. Jack Mendelsohn, *Channing: the Reluctant Radical* (Boston: Little, Brown and Co., 1971).

2. William Henry Channing, *Memoir of William Ellery Channing* (Boston: Wm. Crosby and H. P. Nichols, 1848), p 32.

3. Dag Hammarskjold, *Markings* (New York: Alfred A. Knopf, 1965), p. 205.

CHAPTER 2

What Do I Trust?

What do I trust? What can I rely upon to help me determine what is true and what is right?

We receive much information, many opinions. A variety of authorities would like to convince us that their way is true. But they crowd each other, and it is not clear which interpretation is correct.

This world is a marketplace of values. People with different visions of what is right compete for our allegiance. We see the choices and can justify many options. What can I trust to help me choose that which is right?

Religions are about trust. They point our way through things we cannot fully know.

In some religions trust is centered in a sacred book, such as the Bible or the Koran. In some religions a holy person or a class of holy people interpret the unknown. Others have a code of approved beliefs: a doctrine, a creed, an agreed-upon statement that a person trusts.

Freedom of religious belief is a central affirmation of the Unitarian Universalist tradition. Our trust is not grounded in a sacred book or a holy person or a statement of belief. Rather, we are open to the many forms through which truth and right can be known. We trust this openness over any formula that claims final authority to guide all people in all times. Truth and right, we believe, are most likely to emerge in an environment that encourages us to explore our ideas and convictions.

This principle is fundamental to the liberal religious tradition and can be found in its earliest years. One such occasion took place in

1568. The setting was the town hall of Gyulafehevar in the Eastern
European kingdom of Transylvania, now part of Romania. Represen-
tatives of the four religions of that region were gathered there:
Catholics, Lutherans, Calvinists, and Unitarians.

The occasion was a debate before John Sigismund, King of
Transylvania. This was a time of ferment and intense religious controversy. The Protestant Reformation was spreading, and struggles
between Lutherans and Catholics frequently disrupted the peace.
Religion and politics were intertwined as the Vatican fielded armies
to assert its claims, while the Protestant kings and princes used their
soldiers to transform Catholics into Protestants. I am tempted to claim
that it was a time far different from our own, but then I think of the
struggles between Catholics and Protestants in Northern Ireland, and
the bloodshed among factions of Islam, and the battles between
peoples of opposing sects in India—and the stridency of the religious
right in North America—and I realize that religious strife remains with
us today as when debaters arrived in Gyulafehevar.

At issue was the doctrine of the Trinity: the Christian teaching that
God is three persons: Father, Son, and Holy Spirit. The debate asked
if this doctrine was reasonable. And was it grounded in the Biblical
records?

The debate at Gyulafehevar lasted ten days, with speakers beginning each morning at 5:00 a.m. Into the town hall crowded adherents
of all sides, shouting approval when their team seized an advantage,
grumbling abuse at an unfair remark. Such debates engaged the
people. They were as popular as tournaments and jousts had been in
the Middle Ages. People found the issues under discussion so serious
that those debaters who were judged in error often paid for their faulty
reasoning by imprisonment or even death.

Those on the Unitarian side stated their belief that God is one, not
three as is claimed in the Trinitarian formula. Jesus, they said, should
be regarded as a human being, a teacher, a prophet who has shown
us a way to live on this earth, but he should not be worshipped as God.
The Unitarians argued for tolerance of differences among religious
groups, for the freedom to co-exist with each other as well as the
opportunity to speak without fear of persecution. They asserted that
truth is best determined through reasoned discussion among those
with opposing views. And that there is no benefit to enforcing belief
through coercion.

When the debate ended, King John announced that he would refer the discussions to review by his advisors. Later, he would issue a verdict.

But if we can believe the tradition, many in the audience were won over by arguments advanced by the Unitarian side. The chief spokesman for the Unitarians was a minister named Francis Dávid. It is said that when he returned to his home town after the debate, people lined the streets and greeted him with shouts of praise and joy. According to the historian Earl Morse Wilbur,

> The tradition is that he thereupon mounted a large boulder at the street corner and proclaimed the simple unity of God to them with such persuasive eloquence that they took him on their shoulders and bore him to the great church in the square to continue the theme, and that the whole city accepted the Unitarian faith then and there.[1]

King John Sigismund's verdict on the debate came as a decree. The decree did not proclaim one side or the other right or wrong. It did declare the right of people to follow the belief of their conscience. "Faith is the gift of God," the King stated, "and conscience cannot be forced." Therefore, "We demand that in our dominions there shall be freedom of conscience."[2]

The King's decree forbade one sect from interrupting the worship of another sect, destroying their books, or accosting each other's clergy. Ministers were allowed to preach from their own understandings and interpretations, while church members were free to accept or reject the views of the minister. Thus the right of religious freedom was established throughout the kingdom. No one was to be compelled to a belief that he or she could not in conscience affirm.

This was something new. Other groups had argued for the right to believe and worship as they chose, but they were seeking religious freedom for themselves. Once a minority became the majority, they persecuted the new minorities with vigor, ignoring the cries for religious freedom from those previously in command. But now the King stated a general principle to be protected by law: each person shall have the right to worship according to individual conscience.

King John Sigismund had been convinced by the Unitarian side (and thereby became our only Unitarian king). He came to believe that truth could not be imposed upon people but was most likely to emerge through open consideration and discussion. Therefore, instead of attempting to impose Unitarianism upon his subjects, he granted them religious freedom.

The King was taking a chance. Generally when a sovereign converted, everybody else came along in the deal. The fear was that if competing beliefs were allowed to coexist, truth would be undermined. Chaos would result. But King John Sigismund was stating a different trust, a trust in people to work through issues of truth and right and to make responsible judgments. He hoped that a society in which people were free to follow the dictates of conscience would function and be governable. He proclaimed that it was not the function of government to enforce religious belief but that truth and right were most likely to emerge in a free exchange of ideas, beliefs, and affirmations.

❖ ❖ ❖

Trust in religious freedom is a basic affirmation of the Unitarian Universalist tradition. In determining what is right and true, we place our trust in a process of learning and evaluating through the ongoing exchange of ideas and experiences. For the process to work, there must be an assurance of freedom in which to explore the options.

This is a fine principle when applied to society as a whole. A guarantee of freedom permits individual religious communities to pursue their own approaches to the questions of our lives. Society is enriched by the resulting diversity.

But the Unitarian Universalist claim goes further. It states that individual congregations can be grounded in freedom of belief—that there can be non-dogmatic religious communities. Our churches and fellowships have no creed. There is no statement of belief to which all must assent. The Bible and other books of religious insight are used as resources, but they are not regarded by most Unitarian Universalists as final authority. The influence of the clergy comes from working with people and earning their trust rather than receiving authority by virtue of their position. The community that results is one in which each member is given responsibility to determine what is true and right. Each is encouraged to listen for and to follow the voice of conscience. No one is forced to believe what he or she cannot.

How can the ongoing process of exploring and testing one's belief provide the center for a religious community? Doesn't chaos result, with each person following his or her own idiosyncratic way?

A Unitarian Universalist writes of his search for a congregation where he could express his convictions of truth and right:

What do people do who do not find a place and a people where they belong?

They suffer, that much I know, because for so long I had found no such place and no such people. Not that those whom I knew were not kind and good folk. Not that I had not had a very decent and caring upbringing by parents and other adults who were intelligent and sensitive. Not that I had ever suffered deprivation in a material sense or known great pain. None of these had been part of my experience.

And yet for many years there was a restless emptiness inside me that found no relief that endured more than a few minutes or hours or at most days.

Until a book sale drew me to a Unitarian church on the West Side of Chicago, and a sparkling Southern accent got my attention, and a pamphlet about how this religious community understood religious education all combined to draw me to try yet one more time to see if this could be the place and these the people where I belonged.

I was at that point in my life, thirty-three years of age, with a Doctor of Ministry degree from the University of Chicago and no place to use that degree. I had taken work as a foreign student advisor in frustration at not being able to locate a church/synagogue/temple where I could be honest, be myself, become the person I was striving to be.

My Presbyterian home and rearing had left me theologically without anything. I simply could not accept such doctrines as were part of the requirement for being a minister in that denomination. I knew I cared about religion, deeply, and I knew I had the skills that ministers are supposed to have in order to do the work. But no group, no system, no institution seemed to be for me.

In some fear our family went to Third Unitarian Church that October Sunday to be immediately put at ease by the dress of the people, from casual and even shabby to elegant. This was my kind of place, I could tell that.

I ran into that Southern woman, a Texan, and she remembered me. I later learned she was a believer in Jesus Christ as her Lord and Savior. And I heard during the service from a man of impeccable atheistic credentials, not to speak of the poet who rattled off a few lines of verse at the close of the talk that day (and every Sunday) in keeping with the spirit and content of what had been presented.

The following week a woman from the local neighborhood organization came to share her need for our help, and I was already launched into a seminar on death and dying at the church. Indeed, each event at the church over the next few weeks before I signed the Membership Book in December brought home with greater force and clarity the initial feeling I had on entering Third Unitarian Church in Chicago, a feeling I have heard so many other people express about their encounter with Unitarian Universalism, the feeling that, "I have come home at last."

Kenneth W. Phifer
First Unitarian Universalist Church
Ann Arbor, Michigan

For some, religion is a process of seeking rather than a challenge to follow a particular version of truth. For some, the essence of religion is the awe and wonder that cannot be reduced to a formula. For some, revelation is a continuing process, encountered in the everyday interactions of life, and not restricted to an approved, sanitized revelation. Some people seek a religious community that welcomes and celebrates the diversity of the human condition rather than enforcing conformity.

For such people it does feel like coming home when they find a Unitarian Universalist church or fellowship. Here is a congregation in which members are encouraged to wonder and explore, to ask those questions not allowed in other places, to respond to the voice of conscience even if it may lead to taking unpopular stands.

Here is a congregation where freedom of belief provides an environment that encourages us to examine our faith and explore with each other the questions of what is right and what is true.

It's not completely free. There are guidelines that give form to our freedom. While there is no creed in Unitarian Universalist societies, there are affirmations that guide our seeking.

We already have encountered some of these: the affirmation of human dignity and worth, the valuing of human capacities such as reason and reflection, the recognition of a capacity for moral choice that can be developed in each individual. These have implications for how we approach this question of what we will trust.

For if we affirm human worth and dignity, then we will trust a method for determining right and truth that is open to the thoughts and insights of others. We will trust an approach to decision-making that gives those affected a part in determining policy. We will trust a process that encourages participation and takes into account the effects of decisions upon real, living human beings. We will trust that which shows care for people and compassion.

If we affirm the human ability to reason and to make valid reflections about our experience, then we will trust a decision-making process that encourages us to examine the issues in depth. We will trust an approach to moral concerns that encourages critical discussion, rather than demanding acceptance. We will trust an approach to determining truth that does not shrink before our questions.

And if we do affirm the potential to nourish and develop the human capacity for moral choice, we will protect the right of choice as guided by conscience. We will trust the authentic voice that emerges from a person's struggles as telling us something true, even if we may not agree with that person's conclusions. We will trust the lonely voice of the individual who has seriously grappled with issues of right over the voices of the majority who simply repeat what they have been told.

The Unitarian Universalist theologian James Luther Adams writes,

> The free person does not live by an unexamined faith. To do so is to worship an idol whittled out and made into a fetish. The free person believes with Socrates that the true can be separated from the false only through observation and rational discussion. In this view the faith that cannot be discussed is a form of tyranny.[3]

Many religions claim to value human life. Many speak of serving human dignity and worth. But those affirmations are compromised by an authoritarian structure that presumes to know how best to respond to that dignity and worth. This authority tells the individual what to believe and how to live.

Such an approach undermines the message of human dignity and worth. On one hand we are told that we, as individuals, are of supreme value. But then we are also told that we can't trust our own judgment, conscience, opinions of what is right and wrong. To be faithful to our value as human beings, we must abandon our own perceptions and submit to a higher authority.

It is more consistent to build upon the affirmation of human dignity and worth by affirming that our perceptions and judgments are at least potentially valid by encouraging our capacity for determining right and wrong. Rather than overrule the inner voice, it makes more sense for a religious community to nourish the convictions of conscience and encourage us to heed its call—and stand by us when we do.

If we take seriously the affirmation of human worth and dignity, then it guides our approach to questions of trust. It encourages us to trust ourselves, to make connections with others, to join with people who try to make a difference in the world. With each other, we will learn what is right and what is true.

❖ ❖ ❖

It isn't easy. There are demands made upon those who participate in a community centered in religious freedom, and follow such a path in their lives. We must be willing to doubt, to reconsider. We live with questions that never are fully satisfied.

In such a community we are called to trust ourselves: to build a healthy trust in our own ability to face the challenges of our lives. We must develop our capacity for discernment and judgment and be able to decide when we are right and when we are wrong. We learn to live with those hard choices where no option seems completely right.

In such a community, we are called to trust others. We cannot trust all people always, but choose those with whom we will share the important issues of our lives. Which people will we trust to know our struggles, and which people do we want with us as we encounter the challenges of our days?

In a Unitarian Universalist community, we are called to trust a process of seeking truth and right in which the perceptions of others enrich our own thoughts: a democratic process that encourages us to listen to others as well as state our own views. This process does not resort to decision by decree but encourages people to work together through the choices that we face.

It is a challenge to affirm my own dignity and worth, to trust my ability to take on the decisions of my life. It is a challenge to open myself and to trust others with my concerns. If I have been hurt by others, particularly if they have betrayed my trust, it is a challenge to let myself trust another again. And it is a challenge to trust in a group—to balance my own dignity and worth with others, to work through the issues that come before us with the trust that the problems can be resolved.

Sometimes I feel like Jekyll and Hyde. I just wrote a whole page on how difficult I find it to trust other people in large ways—small ways are easy—but now moments later, I feel differently.

Now I feel that through effort and with a conscious intention, I have come to feel much trust in the good-will of others toward me. It's a matter of not sitting around in what's natural for me—doubt and suspicion—but of going out to test the waters. Will someone come over with some food if I am sick? Will others participate with me in improving social justice and economic opportunities? Will people help me—like me—work with me? Of course they will, and they have. They want to! Why is it that the doubts and suspicions come first to mind?

Leonore Tiefer
The Community Church of New York

The way of freedom is messy. It can be frustrating and tedious to work a decision through a group of independent people. Maybe it would be better to surrender my own judgment to a higher authority.

Except that I don't trust decisions based on appeals to authority or loyalty or tradition. It leaves people out of the process. It does not take into account the circumstances of our lives. We become too easy prey to those who want to assume power by hiding behind the authority of a tradition.

I trust a person who carefully examines the issues and makes an informed choice more than I trust a group that bows to an officially sanctioned view of the true and right. I trust a community of people in which individuals are free to determine the direction of their lives. I trust the often-difficult process of people working together on issues of truth and right.

A religious community based in a trust in the individual's ability to choose—a religious community whose aim is to help develop that capacity—is not as easy as one based in external authority. It's not as popular as a church that promises to take problems away. It's not as neat and efficient as one controlled by a hierarchy.

Yet, I trust it. I trust the people who commit themselves to such an endeavor, and I trust the choices of such a community.

❖ ❖ ❖

A process of determining truth and right that involves participation empowers us. We experience our own dignity and worth.

I was born into a Universalist Church of less than a hundred members in a small southern Wisconsin town. We were a minority in a community of Swiss and German immigrants. Growing up I was proud of our differences but often felt isolated and frustrated trying to explain my religion to my peers.

In the early 1950s I attended a Universalist church camp at Bridgeman, Michigan, where the topic of adult discussion was whether Universalists and Unitarians had enough similarities to merge into one denomination. This was a family church camp so there were many adults, but I was attending alone at age fourteen. It was my first experience away from home, which makes it a vivid memory for me. I felt a sense of a larger church community and realized it was a vibrant religion that existed in many communities.

At one long open discussion about the proposed merger I had listened to adults praise the superiority of both Universalists and Unitarians from their own vantage points, but I couldn't really see any significant difference in basic philosophy. It seemed to me they were only stressing their superficial differences and not looking at the strength to be gained from a larger group. I felt I would need this strength to explain and explore my religion.

So I suddenly found myself addressing the large group meeting on the necessity of a merger from a practical and theological standpoint. As the group listened very attentively to a shy fourteen-year-old, I felt a level of trust and acceptance which I had never experienced before. I'm sure the naive insight of a young person didn't have any great impact on the ultimate decision of the merger, but the opportunity to spontaneously express my views with support and affirmation has bonded me to a lifelong commitment to this denomination. I have found that whatever community I live in I am always comfortable with the people in a Unitarian Universalist church.

Mary Amundsen
First Unitarian Universalist Church
Rochester, Minnesota

We each have insights to share. Each of us can speak with authority. The challenge of religious communities based in freedom of belief is to listen to each other as we each take the risk of sharing our own truths. In that process of sharing and listening, we learn to trust each other—and ourselves.

I recently made a decision which represents a significant step in my life. I signed a Pledge of Resistance, pledging to use legal or illegal demonstration and civil disobedience should U. S. troops invade Central America. The Pledge support group also calls us to educate our fellow citizens about our country's damaging policies in that region.

This is significant because, for years and years, ever since I can remember, while I have voiced and felt strongly about moral issues, I have inevitably taken a back seat of minimal involvement in order to wait and see if maybe, just maybe, authority figures knew something that I didn't. I was always afraid to jump out there in the forefront and to find out I was merely ill-informed and the political leaders knew what they were doing all along. This happened with the Vietnam War, civil rights, and religious freedom in schools. My involvement was not only minimal, but after many of the most significant battles had been fought.

I am stepping out now, trusting my own instincts for right and wrong, making waves, and working with other dedicated citizens, and even changing a few minds around me. I enjoy this new feeling of trusting and acting upon my own instincts, even though it involves some risk-taking. Maybe *because* it involves risk-taking.

Patrick Fleeharty
Unitarian Universalist Church
Anne Arundel County, Maryland

❖ ❖ ❖

Religious freedom is of crucial importance to Unitarian Universalists. We trust the free search for truth and right. In matters of belief and conscience, we will not be compelled to another's truth. In matters of congregational decision-making, we share responsibility for determining the direction of our church or fellowship. In facing the hard choices of our lives, we trust the voice of conscience, informed by the thoughts and experiences of others.

That trust is based in the affirmation that each person can know truth and right. Each shares authority. And so we join together in freedom to seek life's deepest values and to peer into the mystery of existence.

Notes

1. Earl Morse Wilbur, *A History of Unitarianism in Transylvania, England, and America* (Boston: Beacon Press, 1945), p. 38.

2. Ibid.

3. James Luther Adams, *The Prophethood of All Believers* (Boston: Beacon Press, 1986), p. 48.

CHAPTER 3

How Can I Understand God?

There are limits to my ability to determine truth and right, to the control I can exert over my life, to my capacity to perceive and understand. When I reach these limits, I come to the question of God.

I trust my ability to determine what is true. I possess capacities of reason, empathy, understanding. But I also encounter limitations. There are limits to what I can know, understand, articulate. I view the world through my unique perspectives. Truth is larger than what I can conceive.

I trust my ability to determine what is right, and I guide my life by these choices. But here, too, I am aware of limitations. I am capable of deceiving myself by calling forth high moral principles to justify self-interest. I can be insensitive to the issues and concerns of people whose experience is different from my own. Sometimes I'm just plain wrong. Then I must put aside the choices I have made and let myself be guided by a greater good, a deeper right.

I aim for control over my life. I evaluate possibilities; I make plans; I follow the directions I have set. I trust this capacity. I have power to create the person I will be. But this power is not absolute. My attempts to take charge sometimes come apart. I get turned in directions I had not anticipated, and life shows itself as a force stronger than my plans.

When I confront my limitations, when I realize that I am not in full control of my life, when I become aware of a deeper reality moving through me, then I come to the question of God. I wonder what I can believe.

The question of God can be posed in the most ordinary situations. One such occasion took place when I was a junior in college studying in Germany. Soon after arriving, I was traveling alone. I was minimally competent in German—I could order from a menu and arrange for a room—but I couldn't carry on a conversation. At a youth hostel, I tried to talk with a young man who looked to me as if he might speak English. I said, "English?" He said, "No, French." I replied, "Too bad," and walked away.

Later, it occurred to me that this man had answered my question in English. He was not telling me that he couldn't speak English—he was telling me that he was French. My response, "Too bad." It is from such exchanges that international incidents are created.

I didn't try talk to anyone after that. It's a strange experience--after a period of not talking, I felt myself slipping away. I would see myself passing in the reflection of a window and be momentarily surprised.

I was alone in Bavaria on a bus. It was a local bus, and I don't remember why I was on it. But there I was with a few other passengers taking short trips from one little town to the next. Then the bus took on another identity—a school bus. It filled with six- and seven-year-old children who chattered happily with each other. I was surrounded by them as we made our way through the Bavarian countryside.

I must have been an unusual sight: an American in Levis, dusty from too much road, and needing a haircut. But a little German girl took it upon herself to flirt. I'd never been flirted with by a seven-year-old Bavarian, and all I could do was shyly smile back. And then for a moment I was part of everything: the children, the countryside, the bus. For a moment my being as a distinct person was not important. What was important was a common bond that held us together and connected us with life. Our shared existence was all that mattered. I felt both completely insignificant and transformed by a power that was far greater than I.

The bus gradually released its passengers in groups of twos and threes, and I was again aware of myself as a solitary traveler in a foreign land. I must have made it to my destination that day, but I don't remember. I do remember that moment of connectedness and transformation.

When I recall that experience, the memory brings me strength and hope. It also brings me to wonder why it felt so important and what it could mean. For a moment I peered into the mystery underlying existence, and that awakened in me the question of God.

What can I believe about God? How can I conceive of the force that pulses through my being—the force that creates and sustains life? Throughout the history of our movement, religious liberals have peered into the mystery of God and created images to represent what they have found.

The Unitarians of the late 1700s and early 1800s found an underlying order. They perceived a universe constructed according to rational plan by a "benevolent deity whose concern was with the happiness of his creatures."[1] Humanity, said the Unitarians, is made in the image of this God. In our rationality, then, is something of the divine. In our concern for each other, we express qualities embedded in creation.

The Unitarians contrasted their God of order, rationality, and benevolence with the God of orthodoxy. The orthodox encountered the mystery of existence and perceived a different reality. They found a God with absolute power over creation, a God inaccessible to human understanding and experience. We cannot question the ways of God, said the orthodox, we can only submit. The happiness of His creatures was not a concern of the orthodox God. The aim of life, rather, was salvation, and salvation did not lie in our hands. It was conferred by God, without concern for the accomplishments or goodness of the individual's life. To the Unitarians such a God was arbitrary and tyrannical and, well, inhumane.

For the Unitarians there was no discontinuity between the human world and that of God. Divine virtue was reflected in human virtue. Divine order was reflected in the order of life in this world. Divine rationality provided the structure of existence. The effect was to encourage individuals to develop their potential—to pursue their perceptions of virtue and order—for in so doing they were drawing upon God-given talents. Unitarians of the early nineteenth century were independent people, confident in the human ability to make a difference in this world, fiercely devoted to the free search for truth. Salvation, they believed, could be attained through conscientious and humane work in this world.

The religion of the early Unitarians was a fine and free faith, but soon it was challenged by a new generation within the Unitarian movement. Your God, they said, is too cold, too impersonal, too abstract, too rational. This does not represent the mystery of existence as we perceive it. It leaves out passion, creativity, inspiration; it misses the importance of poetry, literature, music—the things that feed the spirit; it misses the depths of human experience—both ecstasy and grief. And so Transcendentalism was born in revolt against a too orderly and too abstract worldview. The Transcendentalists perceived God as a life-giving spirit that flowed through everyday experience, as Ralph Waldo Emerson said, in "the blowing clover and the falling rain."[2] They were suspicious of the rites and formalities of religion and sought, instead, direct experience of that force which brings us life. "It is an intuition," proclaimed Emerson. "It cannot be received at second hand." The Transcendentalists saw God as part of each person's life and each person a part of God. "I grow in God," Emerson wrote, "I am only a form of Him. He is the soul of me. I can even with a mountainous aspiring say, I am God."

There was considerable controversy between the early Unitarians, with their rational God, and the Transcendentalists, with their God of intuition. That tension has continued throughout the history of the Unitarian Universalist movement. A tradition of rationalism remains with adherents who seek to penetrate the mysteries of creation through reason and understanding. And a tradition of mysticism remains with adherents who seek direct experience of the holy.

It may seem unlikely that people from such differing perspectives would camp under the same tent, but both groups challenge religious orthodoxy. Orthodoxy begins with the assumption of revelation. The orthodox proclaim that the essence of God has been revealed with a particular event or message. To them, our task as human beings is to respond to that revelation and to guide our lives by its truth.

The rationalist, however, questions revelation. "How can it be that this event is closed to our investigation? How can we say that truth is so confined?" Doctrine is fair game for reasoned evaluation. So we challenge orthodox teachings that hurt people or are unjust or don't make sense. We believe that probing life's mystery is an ongoing process, never final or complete.

The religious person who seeks direct intuition of the spirit also questions orthodox assertions of final revelation. For the voice of God can still be perceived in everyday experience. If that voice points in directions other than those indicated by tradition or doctrine, so be it. The living God must take precedence over the God that has been tamed and adjusted for human purposes.

What can I believe about God? The liberal religious tradition offers these two directions. It encourages me to think rationally about concepts of God, and to listen to the voice of intuition. The question of God, then, becomes open to investigation and experience.

One Unitarian Universalist writes of his wondering about God after returning home from the funeral of his brother, who had been killed in an automobile accident.

> After the funeral I met a high school friend. The words his mother spoke on the porch sincerely were meant to be comforting when she said, "It was God's will." And they were taken in that spirit.
>
> But something was wrong.
>
> A man still in his twenties, with a wife and two small children, was killed by a drunk driver. It was God's will. A man with a sense of humor, with an easy-going nature, with a number of friends. God's will. A man from whom no harm could come. This was God's will?
>
> I had to think about it. No, I had to feel it, had to reach back into my Bible training. I had to analyze events, I had to put things into perspective, and I had to understand it....
>
> No, I still do not understand it, and I don't know if I can ever learn to even through my questioning. But I have learned to question.
>
> *Jim Cubberly*
> *Dupage Unitarian Church*
> *Naperville, Illinois*

We question our own ideas of God and those of other traditions. Questioning is not infidelity but a faith that life's mysteries can be penetrated, that a concept of God can be strong enough to survive our wondering.

Another Unitarian Universalist writes of her intuition of a force that comforts and reassures—an intuition that addresses her own questioning.

> For many years before my first pregnancy, my mind felt cramped with anxiety because there were so many questions I hadn't found answers for.
>
> I worked until the sixth month of pregnancy. It was summer

and my baby was due in November. My husband and I rented a cabin in the Muskokas for one week. It was comfortable and only a few feet away from the lake.

One morning I woke early, dressed, made tea and went out to sit on the white painted wood chair by the lake. I felt the morning air greet me as though I were its first visitor. For the next few minutes the lake, with its surrounding pines and hills, belonged to me.

I was free from a weight I expected to carry for the rest of my life, free from that anxiety, and my lungs drew in a quiet joy. For the first time I realized how naturally insignificant my ego was and how significant my life was. If I were to die that afternoon, all the beauty surrounding me would still be there.

This new revelation calmed me like the promise of eternal life. If I could see these gentle greens that sculptured the lake and the sky, if I could respond to this message, then surely it was a part of me. If I inhaled this air, then my breath would fly in the wind to be carried off across the lake, above the trees, over the hills to another lake, and a part of me would be somewhere I couldn't see. If I were part of something I couldn't see, it must be OK to ask questions and not have the answers.

Janet I. Vickers
Don Heights Unitarian Congregation
Scarborough, Ontario

Reason and intuition are both tools available to me in my seeking. Both guide me as I seek to determine what I can believe about God.

❖ ❖ ❖

Religious liberalism encourages us to wonder about God. Throughout our tradition we have drawn various images to represent the force of being that flows through our lives.

In the Universalist side of our tradition, people looked to the mystery of existence and found a God of love. They rebelled at orthodox concepts of a punishing God and in particular disputed the teaching that the world is divided into two groups: the saved and the damned. The orthodox claimed that the saved will be granted eternal bliss, but the damned will find eternal misery.

Is this any way for a good and loving God to behave? The Universalists thought not. Their God was supportive, caring, forgiving, ultimately concerned for the welfare of humanity. The Universalists believed in universal salvation—a teaching that disputes the idea that humanity is divided into the saved and the damned. Instead, said the Universalists, all are saved. All are interconnected. All are one.

The effect of this Universalist affirmation was to view the source of being as trustworthy and supportive. Through the successes and failures of everyday existence, we are exposed to truth and right. We can learn how better to lead our lives and to be faithful to a loving God. This message is similar to that of the early Unitarians and Transcendentalists. That is, the encounter with "the mysterious" is ongoing. Again, revelation and doctrine are not final. We are, rather, instructed in ways of living. We are guided by a loving force.

In the early twentieth century, the humanist movement introduced another approach. The humanists, with representatives both in Unitarian and Universalist churches, looked into mystery and found an indifferent universe. It was neither good nor evil, neither supportive nor punishing. Our response, said the humanists, must be a conscious affirmation of human value and of life. The measure of our beliefs and our ethics must be the effects upon human beings.

We must live, said the humanists, by that which enhances human life. We must resist whatever demeans humanity. Humanists are particularly critical when religious enthusiasms hurt rather than help people, such as, the centuries of religious wars when Christians have killed and maimed each other over disagreements about doctrine. For the religious humanist, it is absurd for doctrine to be more important than the actual lives of men and women. They insist that we create a context for life in which people with differences can coexist and which nourishes human growth and possibility.

Unitarian Universalist Christians offer another response to the mysterious. For the Christians within our movement, God is best known through the example and teachings of Jesus. Jesus, say the Unitarian Universalist Christians, is not a god to be worshipped. He is, rather, a teacher and prophet and exemplar whose guidance we may follow in seeking to live most fully. The biblical witness offers continuing wisdom and guidance to those who want to live in relationship to God.

What distinguishes Unitarian Universalist Christianity is that it is not based in a creed or restricted by doctrine. Faith assumes the nature of a pilgrimage. The Unitarian Universalist Christian asks us to respond to Jesus as a person and discover what his life can tell us about our own. When we approach him with openess and trust, then we will find our own lives made new.

Our encounter with life's mystery is ongoing, and Unitarian Universalists continue to create images to express our experience. We continue to be informed and enriched by others who pursue similar concerns.

Feminist theologians have contributed to our image-making with their sense of the world as interconnected and interdependent. Rather than citing a father God who creates a separate world, the feminist theologians express their vision in the language of the whole—the masculine and feminine shared. The holy is not apart from the world but flows through all life.

The Eastern religions—Hinduism, Buddhism, Taoism—show us that the religious enterprise is an ongoing journey. In the Eastern religions, beliefs are not the primary reality, since what a person believes at one stage of the journey may not be true or appropriate at another stage. There is an affirmation of the quest that each person pursues throughout his or her life. Eastern religion also has a sense of the interdependence of all things and all experience. Each action produces effects that ripple throughout creation.

For years Native American religion was felt to be the primitive ideas of a people ripe for conversion to Christianity. Only recently have we awakened to the beauty of its message: the natural world gives us roots and nourishes those who acknowledge and respect and goodness of nature. Chief Luther Standing Bear writes,

> The old people came literally to love the soil and they sat or reclined on the ground with a feeling of being close to a mothering power. It was good for the skin to touch the earth and the old people like to remove their moccasins and walk with bare feet on the sacred earth. Their tipis were built upon the earth and their altars were made of earth....The soil was soothing, strengthening, cleansing, and healing.[3]

An image invoked in the Unitarian Universalist statement of purposes and principles is the interdependent web of existence. It pledges, "respect for the interdependent web of existence of which we are a part." This image suggests that each of us is part of a whole. Whatever one person does affects that whole. The "web" also affects each of us: shaping our lives, guiding us, relating us to that which is greater than self. We are dependent upon it as it is affected by the choices we make. Relationship, then, becomes the essential reality of existence.

I seek relationship with that interdependent web of existence. I try to live in response to its mystery. Sometimes I am shaken by the encounter as it reveals the narrowness of my vision. And sometimes I am renewed, given strength and hope when I become aware of that force of life at the center of being.

❖ ❖ ❖

The encounter with the mysterious yields experiences upon which a faith can be built. The interdependent web connects us with life and reveals its truths.

One person experienced the mysterious as a reality greater than herself.

This is about childbirth. It was in 1942, long before Lamaze or anything of the kind. It was not good manners to talk about intimate things, and while I had all the technical information, I did not know what to expect. I was very happy about the baby, and I was not afraid. I thought if others can live through it, I can too.

The pains started and were quite bearable. The pains got harder, and for a few minutes I had the feeling, "Do you really want to go through with this?" And then, suddenly, I had no more time to think of my pain. I was taken along by something tremendous that was happening to me, in me, through me. It was an experience that does not compare to anything else....I don't know why it happened to me, of all people.

Else Baer
Unitarian Fellowship
Muttontown, New York

Another person experiences a force of being that renews life in nature and in oneself.

> Nature teaches me about trust. I'm continuously amazed at how deforested areas rejuvenate themselves within a few seasons after fire or other natural destruction. Jungles which have been macheted away can almost be observed growing back to claim their territories. I'm always impressed by my body's ability to heal itself after surgery or a wound. These observations built up my trust in life itself.
>
> *Eleanor Hill*
> *Unitarian Church*
> *Cherry Hill, New Jersey*

For yet another, a deeply felt connection with the universe brings great joy.

> I have always felt a sense of 'at-one-ness' with the Universe from childhood—experiencing an inexplicable fullness of joy and radiating love for the good earth and all that abounds therein; for all the creatures of the earth.
>
> My exposure to the religion of the black church and my experience as a black person affected me deeply and translated itself into a yearning and a commitment to "lend a helping hand" to my fellow travelers—so I became a nurse and in the course of my work came into a fuller appreciation of the majesty and beauty of humankind. Always I am led to sing a poem of praise for all that is.
>
> *Helene A. Lightborne*
> *The Community Church of New York*

One woman shares the experience of reaching limits. Her plans are changed by the circumstances of life, and she is forced to let go of her attempts at control. In so doing she encounters a reality greater than her own plans, and discovers a transforming dimension to existence.

> My only child—my son, whom I raised alone—came close to death. Many words have been spoken about the unnaturalness of your child going before you, the preciousness of life, and ap-

preciation of simple moments of beauty. These have become very real to me.

But there's more—and the sequence has made me more respectful of the spiritual components of life.

Like many of the middle-class working force, I work very hard. A workaholic to be exact. If there's time left in the day after doing my best on the job and keeping my house running efficiently, I might pamper myself, i.e., have a warm bath, read, or call a friend.

Well, the degree to which my time was blocked off with Things That Needed To Be Done came to a grinding halt.

While at work I broke my right wrist. I went from a life of constant productivity to an inability to do almost everything. Try opening a jar, tying shoes, chopping vegetables, etc., with only your non-dominant hand. What I could do was read, visit, and listen to music. I had a graphic, powerful, and immediate contrast from my compulsive work style to a life of forced leisure.

Somewhere in the midst of the two seemingly negative experiences, I developed a spiritual dimension, lacking earlier. I was a devout agnostic until then. Now I have a God. My God has no gender, rather, It is a positive force around all of us. We can use It if we choose. This Spiritual Force is helping me grow, though I had the option to wallow in self pity —"Why did this happen to me?"—had I chosen a different course.

It's time to get on with my dreams, do the things now that have always been for the future. I can't take life and health for granted any more. I am transforming from a super achiever to a multidimensional person. The change is exciting.

Donna Marjorie Wilson
Los Angeles, California

I am drawn to a belief in a force of being in which we participate, and which we affect by the choices we make—a larger reality that flows through my life and that I share with the people and the living things of this earth. This God calls us to transcend the limitations of personal vision and to seek connections with the interdependent web of existence. To do so renews and transforms and makes us whole.

What difference does it make to hold such a view of God? How does it change me? How does it affect the life of a religious community?

There are, to me, many implications. Religious liberals focus not only on a person's individual salvation or relationship to God. Rather, we emphasize that one person is not saved at the expense of the rest. Our fates are tied inextricably together; when one person suffers, his or her cries travel throughout the web of existence. As Psalm 82 says, "All the foundations of the earth are shaken when the weak and the needy are deprived of justice." We try not to forget the poor, the hungry, the homeless, those caught in crossfire between warring groups.

We are concerned not simply for the good of our own community, family, friends. We consider the fate of those outside our immediate experience—those of different nations, cultures, creeds. We seek to understand each other, to build bridges between people, to work together toward shared interests and common concerns. We affirm the mosaic of human experience—the colors, the varying shapes, the patterns—and celebrate the richness of its diversity.

We teach our children about the peoples of the world—their joys, their sufferings, the meanings they find in their lives. We encourage our children to be curious about children whose lives are different from theirs and help them feel kinship with people of different cultures who pursue meanings different from theirs. We emphasize that all of us are part of the same world, that we share a common humanity. We teach our children to regard each human being as special and deserving respect.

And we extend our vision beyond the human community to our relationship with the earth. As Wendell Berry has observed, "It is impossible to care for each other more or differently than we care for the earth....There is an uncanny resemblance between our behavior toward each other and our behavior toward the earth." We are grateful for the gift of life shared among the inhabitants of this fragile planet.

With such a view of God, we are encouraged to participate in life to the fullest—to be engaged, committed, to invest our talents in making a difference in this world. Through involvement, we open ourselves to change and to the transforming power of God.

William F. Schulz, president of the Unitarian Universalist Association, writes:

> Only in communion with that larger tapestry of which we are a part can we be changed, transformed, made whole. And what is amazing is that tapestry of hope and possibility is always changing too, dynamic, responsive, ever being born. In this sense God does not exist but is always being born.[4]

❖ ❖ ❖

Sometimes I meet people whose beliefs pervade their lives and who demonstrate how it is to live in relationship with God.

One such person was eighty-seven years old, a member of the congregation I served. She rarely attended Sunday morning services because of health problems, but as we talked she showed an interest and involvement in life that I often find among long-time Unitarian Universalists.

She told me of the books she had been reading, the ideas she was wondering about, the times she had had to rethink issues and change her mind. We talked about the illnesses she struggled with, her weakening vision and how sometimes she felt so tired. She told me that she would close her eyes and imagine a green meadow with water flowing through it and that the scene was soothing and healing. She was working on a painting of that scene, she said, because she wanted to keep it before her. It connected her to something deep within.

Then her tone changed, and she sparkled as she told me of her grandchildren and the trip west she recently had taken with her family and the next one she was planning. And as we talked I knew why she was a Unitarian Universalist: a characteristic involvement in life, an openness and hope.

She told me how she decided to join the Unitarian Universalist church many years before. She was going back and forth between two congregations, but she noticed that in the other church, she often found herself sitting in a clenched position—as if protecting herself. But one morning she was in the Unitarian Universalist church and looked at the position into which her hands were resting. They were open, accepting, trusting, seeking to be filled. At that point she decided she was a Unitarian Universalist.

Among Unitarian Universalists I have found many people with similar attitudes. They are curious—open to life's mystery. They trust life. They seek to be filled. It is a central theme of our tradition: by living with openness and affirmation, by participating fully in life, we are transformed.

❖ ❖ ❖

I struggle with God. I lose faith. I fall out of relationship with the interdependent web of existence.

Sometimes I trust only my own perceptions and consider only my own ends. I forget that there are limits to my knowledge, that security is never total and that human power always is subject to greater forces of existence. I try to live only by my powers, but they are not enough.

Sometimes I am reluctant to enter into relationships. Relationships change people, and I don't want to be changed. I want the familiar and comfortable, and I would just as soon not deal with the unknown. I stand back, not trusting the always-changing flow of existence.

And sometimes I hold on to life too tightly. I cling to meanings I have created, even as they crumble. I try to control people when they need to grow on their own. I can't bear to abandon goals and ambitions even when they no longer are appropriate. I refuse to let go, to relax, to open myself to the mysteries of existence.

But then I feel myself becoming cut off from life. My strength drains. I am not renewed. I become a partial being. I try to be fully in charge, but I separate myself from the spiritual part of life that is not subject to my careful control.

During my first years in the ministry, I encountered people who were in pain. I shared hard times with them. I was part of their lives as some endured tragedy and as others faced the everyday discouragements that wear people down. I wanted to heal them and make their pain go away, but I could not. I wanted to protect them from life, but they could not be protected. And so I despaired of the suffering in this world and how helpless we each are. I despaired of my ability to be a minister.

But then I began to realize that people did not expect me to protect or save them. They did not want a savior but someone to be with them as they encountered their pain. These people suffered, but they remained engaged in life, and they could still smile. They didn't expect me to heal them, because life itself heals.

Life heals. Life renews. I don't have to make it happen. I can't make it happen. When I let myself fall out of relationship, I forget that we live in an interdependent web that heals us, transforms us, and makes us whole. I am called, then, to seek relationship with mystery, with the interdependent web of existence and, therefore, with life itself.

What, then, can I believe about God?

I believe that I participate in a larger life force that is accessible to reason and experience. This force relates me to life: to my neighbors, to other peoples, to the world of nature. Being so related saves me from my isolation, opens me to the suffering and the joy, the pain and the wonder of existence. I participate in existence to the fullest. In so doing, I am changed. I am awakened to life.

Notes

1. Conrad Wright as quoted in David Robinson, *The Unitarians and the Universalists* (Westport, CT: Greenwood Press, 1985), p. 22.

2. Ralph Waldo Emerson, as quoted in David Parke, *The Epic of Unitarianism* (Boston: Beacon Press, 1957), p. 108.

3. Chief Luther Standing Bear, *Land of the Spotted Eagle* (Boston: Houghton Mifflin Co., 1933).

4. William F. Schulz, *The World* (March/April, 1987).

CHAPTER 4

Where Can I Find Meaning?

What matters in life? What has worth and deserves my commitment?

Sometimes I feel the question of meaning as an experience of something missing. A restless discontent warns me that I am squandering days. I waste life on things that don't matter.

I speak with a person, but it seems that we don't connect. Our words do not reach each other, we are not nourished by the contact, and I walk away feeling frustrated. Or I go through a day in which I am busy doing tasks and pursuing goals, but I wonder if they are worth the effort. An unrest inside drives me toward questions of meaning.

On other occasions an experience of life's fullness raises the question of meaning. I find something that matters. Here is a promise to life that I have only begun to realize.

I convinced an old man to leave the security of his room one day and take a walk outside with me—it may have been his first time out in years. As he blinked at the sun's brightness and exclaimed at how the trees had grown and greeted each person who passed, I was certain that this event had meaning. A young mother came to my office carrying her baby. She told me about this child's twin, who died at birth and how the baby she was carrying almost didn't survive. She talked about how much this child means to her—how he seems a gift. I had never seen this woman before, and I don't expect to see her again. But in that conversation I was connected to her and her struggles and in the process I felt related to life itself. In that conversation was meaning.

Often I find myself caught between choices. I look for direction toward meaning and the opportunity to pursue its promise.

Religion guides us in questions of meaning. It helps us determine what is worthy. As a Unitarian Universalist I am indebted to the Jewish and the Christian traditions for stories and images that direct me toward things that matter.

From the Jewish tradition comes the story of Moses, who led his people out of slavery and toward a land where they could be true to the covenant they had made with God. It was a place where they could live by their own standards and worship according to their beliefs. This land would flow with "milk and honey" as they would be free to affirm their own truth and follow their own vision.

For me as a Unitarian Universalist, this story is not just of a single people in a particular time. Rather, the story of the Israelites who left Egypt and were tested by many temptations is the story of all oppressed people. It is our own story as we seek to be free. It tells of our struggle against those who oppress, it warns of our vulnerability to false gods, it describes our failures of heart when confronted with setbacks and trials.

This ancient story is retold whenever people seek liberation. It is told again when those on the bottom of society recognize their own dignity and try to make a new place for themselves. It is the story of an individual who is poor or of a minority group who has withstood the blows of life—but who undertakes his or her own journey to the promised land. It is the story of a person addicted to drugs or alcohol who seeks courage to confront whatever is destroying his or her life. And it is the story of the American middle class as we struggle with the false idols that clutter our paths and keep us from realizing the full promise of humanness.

The struggle has meaning. As a Unitarian Universalist who affirms inherent human dignity and worth, I celebrate and offer whatever help I can when people undertake this journey. Even if the struggle is not immediately successful, even if time and time again we are tested—the struggle is worthy.

We raise our cups during the celebration of the Passover seder, and in community we acknowledge our kinship with those who are oppressed. We remind ourselves that their battles are ours—that these are humanity's struggles. We acknowledge kinship with each person who journeys toward his or her own promised land.

In a seder written for Unitarian Universalists, David Weissbard declares,

Brothers and sisters, we have been remembering our slavery and our liberation. But just as it was we, and not our ancestors only, who were liberated in Egypt, so it is we, not our ancestors only, who live in slavery. Our slavery is not over and our liberation is not complete. The task of liberation is long, and it is work we ourselves must do.[1]

In the Christian tradition, we find the story of Jesus of Nazareth, whose message startled his hearers. He stated that the Kingdom of God, which they had so long awaited, already was among them. It was present and coming into being.

The old world is passing away, Jesus taught. The new truths of the Kingdom of God challenge us to love our neighbors as ourselves, for all people are related. We welcome the poor and despised at our tables for these people too are part of the Kingdom. In this new Kingdom of God, we even love our enemy—we recognize our relationship with that person who wants to destroy us.

In the Kingdom of God, we do not emulate the "respectable" people who are so busy that they ignore the traveler left bleeding on the road. Rather, we follow the example of the Samaritan who recognized the traveler as a brother and offered him care. And if to follow the new truths, we must break some of society's rules—if to feed the hungry we must harvest on the Sabbath—then we must. For we live with the greater reality of the Kingdom of God that now is coming into being.

The teachings of Jesus challenge me as a Unitarian Universalist. They tell me of a reality greater than my personal needs and desires, and they relate me to a deeper vision of what it is to be human. Here are things of worth.

We gather as Unitarian Universalist congregations at Easter to celebrate the new life that overcomes death. We see it in the change of the seasons, the life that emerges from the cold and bleakness of winter. We see it in a person who takes risks to help a neighbor. We see it in each man or woman who participates in life with affirmation and hope, despite the ever-present threat of failure and defeat. For then death is overcome, the new being comes forth, life is transformed. At Easter we gather to acknowledge our relationship to the force of life that transforms and renews.

I look to the stories of the world's religions to instruct me about things of worth. These stories contain the wisdom of generations who have sought to articulate meaning. In the Christian and Jewish traditions, in the religions of the East, in the faith of the Native Americans, there are resources to guide me in my search.

❖ ❖ ❖

There are different ways to use these resources. In religious orthodoxy, the starting point for determining meaning is found in the traditions of the faith. The religious institution defines what is most worthy. The challenge to the faithful, then, is to direct their lives according to these creeds and practices.

Religious liberalism, however, approaches questions of meaning from another perspective. It urges us to become involved, to invest ourselves in life, to take risks. It encourages us to be active participants as we discover and define what is worthy. The wisdom of the world's religions—as well as of our own tradition—may guide us, but the ultimate decisions are ours.

And so I look to my own experiences. I remember occasions when I have found meaning.

When I was a college student, I was hit by a car. I was walking to a movie and came to an intersection with roads coming in five directions and lights pointing five ways. I read the wrong set of lights, saw the cars stopping, and walked. But the stopped cars were in a left-turn lane. Those moving straight ahead had the green light. I stepped past a car that had stopped and into the path of a driver who had no warning.

It could have been a serious accident. It wasn't. My bills came to ten dollars, but I did hundreds of dollars of damage to the car. My head broke the windshield, which had to be replaced; my head didn't. I did suffer some damage to my pride. The local newspaper's account reported that "Marshall was apparently confused by the signs." For the rest of my college career, that line was read back to me.

I walked around campus for a few weeks with my arm in a sling, hurting all over. I felt vulnerable—the memory of the car's impact took long to fade. I also felt stupid. It's embarrassing enough to be hauled away in an ambulance, without also knowing that my bad judgment caused the commotion. I would have preferred to be an innocent victim.

Every once in a while, as I limped around, someone would approach me and express concern and ask how I was doing. Some of these people I knew only vaguely, some not at all. Yet I was touched by their attention, and I was surprised at how much it meant to me. I hadn't thought that a few simple words could make a difference.

Twenty years have passed since that event, and I have long since forgotten the doctors and nurses who treated me for my injuries. But I still remember the people who offered their attention and concern. Their words had meaning. I was drawn out of the isolation imposed by my hurt, my self-consciousness, and my embarrassment. These people brought me out of myself and into relationship with a wider human community of support and forgiveness. Through this relatedness I was healed. It made a difference.

I look to the experience of other Unitarian Universalists. What do they find to be of worth? Where do they experience meaning?

I find meaning in close and intimate relationships with people. When I share my thoughts, concerns, confusions, frustrations, anger, joy, and love with another person it usually has been followed by that person sharing his or her own inner thoughts and feelings. That sharing has made a difference in my life and in most cases it has touched the other person's life too. There are times when it affirms me, times when it enlightens me, and times when it devastates me. But almost always there has been a lesson learned that makes a difference in my decisions, behavior, or attitudes.

To me, intimate sharing is a way of saying, "I care about you. You are valuable to me." Intimate relationships offer me the opportunity to care about another person and to receive that same caring. It is what matters in my life most.

Christine Washburn
Unitarian Church
Rockville, Maryland

This spring our Social Responsibility Committee got involved for the first time in an area project that feeds the homeless and hungry of Trenton. I volunteered and showed up for orientation on time and a little uneasy. Would I do what I was supposed to? Would the suffering of the people be too painful for me?

The time flew! It was hard, hot work on a very steamy day. After three hours I was soaking wet and exhilarated. I tried to explain to my sister that evening what a great day it was. Her response was "Oh, the do-gooder syndrome." She was wrong. The task was meaningful, and from that came the exhilaration.

Michelle Hunt
Unitarian Universalist Church
Titusville, New Jersey

I find meaning when I'm trusted and let inside a new world. I found it when R____ shared with me late one night two hours of graphic detail of his torture in the hands of the South African police. It was the first time, as he told me later, that he'd ever talked of it.

I found it when B____ sent me a long, beautifully insightful letter from prison sharing his innermost thoughts. I knew that through building trust I had made a difference in his life—that maybe I had helped him choose life.

I feel it when I listen to countless stories of trial, suffering, courage, and commitment to a greater good and to overcoming heavy odds.

Charlotte McPherson
The Community Church of New York

What I think provides the greatest excitement and meaning for me about living is a deep sharing with another person. Sometimes it's just a look, a smile, a chemistry that connects two souls for a moment. Often it involves a shared emotion: anxiety, love, fear, anger, sadness. It could be a physical experience: completing a marathon, building a house, mowing the lawn, making love. It could be intellectual: discussing an idea, planning a task, designing the future.

The common denominator is sharing.

Bob Slawson
Unitarian Universalist Fellowship
Huntington, New York

About two years ago, I found myself in the bottom of a very deep depression. At various times I felt a strong pull toward driving off the road with the intention of seeking a simple solution. I internalized; I sought no one—except my wife. Her response, once she realized the seriousness of my state, became one of support. She spoke with others—our minister, for one.

Eventually I managed, by myself and the support of others, to pull out. As I was able to talk about that period, I realized those things which turned me around. I had lost any sense of intelligent rationale—except one. Every time I felt like giving in (and up), I envisioned my daughter. I realized not simply my responsibility to her but also my responsibility in what I had established as a human being.

Later, when I spoke to close friends, I found their concern to be overwhelming. I was asked (and told) not to exclude them— to seek their support before I reached such a stage again.

The response of my family and friends put much into perspective. Yet, and it is never reached such proportions since, I felt a sense of the struggles of others (which are not always successful). Basically, I realized that I am not a single being, but that I am joined with others. I need, I think we all need, to seek and to use this realization.

Anonymous

A theme that runs through Unitarian Universalist efforts to determine what matters in life is that meaning is found in relationship: to each other, to a community of caring and support, to the deeper flow of life. When I find myself falling out of relationship, life becomes empty. I neglect the people close to me. I become obsessed with my own concerns and ignore the struggles of others. I get lost in myself and take life for granted. But in relationship I find myself guided to things of worth.

Involvement in the community becomes important: the religious community, the local community, the larger human community. Through involvement in community we are joined with each other as we try to make a difference in society. We temper our individual interests and pursue a shared vision of what is right and good. We determine and pursue common missions as we take responsibility for the society we are a part of.

Involvement in each other's lives becomes important. My life is affected by people with whom I come into contact and by many whom I will never meet. I also am nourished and supported and renewed through sharing with other people. I try to live with care for others and with respect. I try to do my part to help people and find meaning in being engaged.

Involvement in the world of nature becomes important. Here are the forces that give us life, the earth in which our lives are centered. Here are the creatures with whom we share this planet. Our personal fates cannot be neatly separated from those of the other beings of this earth. Our futures are intertwined. Hence, there is meaning in giving attention to the world of nature and letting ourselves be nourished by it.

Openness to the transforming forces of existence also becomes important. It comes to people in different ways. For some, music is a language that expresses a transforming power. Others find relationship through prayer or meditation. For still others it is through the ongoing engagement with the world. And for some it is the experience of creativity, bringing elements together in new ways. In each there is relatedness to a transforming force.

In *Spirituality for Ministry,* Urban T. Holmes defines spirituality as our openness to relationship. In a Unitarian Universalist context, spirituality is not separated from the world, with its temptations and joys. Spirituality, rather, is found in participation—being together with our sisters and brothers, affirming what we hold in common, staying open to the larger forces of existence. It is a spirituality of embracing the world.

Through engagement in life I find things of worth.

❖ ❖ ❖

For me, the liberal religious approach to meaning begins in relationship. It encourages us to be active participants in life. The world's religions offer guidance, but ultimately we determine things of worth by involving ourselves in life's challenges and opportunities.

One implication of this approach emerges in our Unitarian Universalist children's programs. Religious education in a liberal religious community is not the same as in orthodoxy. We proceed from different assumptions and aim toward different ends.

The traditional manner of religious education is to teach children the forms of faith: prayers, rituals, the creed. The children may not understand what they're getting, but the assumption is that as they get older, they will. As they grow older, it is hoped, the forms they have learned will gather meaning.

The liberal religious approach reverses that system. We start not with forms but with participation, not with statements of belief but with relationship. Rather than teach children prayers and rituals, we start with experiences that have meaning for them. We start with whatever children wonder about: experiences of nature—the colored leaves of autumn, the cold and snow of winter, the miracle of plants that grow; experiences of the mystery of life—a newborn kitten, hatching chickens, a baby; experiences of pain and sickness, encounters with death. Experiences of imagination, dreaming, times when our thoughts conceive things we cannot see. Experiences of relatedness to family, friends, community. Experiences of loneliness, sadness, the times when life does not proceed as we wish.

As a child I attended Sunday School at the Unitarian Church of Quincy, Illinois. My class was small: three regulars, two or three others who were there sometimes. Class consisted of reading the stories in the books and talking about them with the teacher. We did not have the variety of programs offered today.

Nonetheless, something stuck. My early religious teaching has shaped the way I approach issues of religion and meaning. Religion, for me, is a wider ranging phenomenon than it is for others. In my view, religion has to do with the process of wondering and valuing and finding meaning in life. It has to do with the relationships we form, the choices we make. It has to do with the feeling of mystery and awe that sometimes comes over us, and the affirmation that life is of worth, even when we don't know why.

Religion is woven through all life. It's not just what happens on Friday night or Sunday morning. It doesn't have to take place in a particular place regarded as sacred. And it may not fit into an approved set of beliefs and traditions.

Sometimes a person says to me, "I'm just not religious." But then this person talks about his or her struggles to live ethically and of the wonder he or she finds in nature and of concerns for the future of this planet—and the statement of not being religious doesn't make sense. It doesn't make any more sense than those who claim they are religious by following certain rituals and stating certain beliefs but do nothing to contribute to the life we share.

When I go to a place or attend an event that is defined as religious, I often find that it is anything but. People are dressed up, doing things I don't understand, telling unlikely tales—and I don't see how this can be religious, since it has no meaning. It is unrelated to the rest of people's lives.

Religion must be centered in what has meaning. And meaning is discovered and created in relationship. This approach runs through Unitarian Universalist programs from religious education for children to theology classes for adults. It changes our way of "doing religion." It changes us as we engage in the ongoing process of investing ourselves in people and experiences and discoveries.

❖ ❖ ❖

In what do I find meaning? Unitarian Universalists answer the question in different ways. We have different interests, concerns, and experiences. A theme that joins us is that of seeking meaning through becoming engaged in life.

To live in relationship does not necessarily bring security or certainty. It does not permit us to nail meanings down. I never can relax in the confidence that now I've got it figured out. But this perspective keeps me open to life. Through seeking relationship, I participate in events that matter.

Three representatives of our church met with the editor of the city's newspaper. A member of the church had committed suicide after a difficult life. She had been loved within the congregation. People had reached out to her, but it had not been enough. Her past weighed too heavily and ultimately brought her down.

The local newspaper had made this woman's misery its lead story on the front page. Her suicide shouted from the headline. And so the three of us met with the editor to tell him our distress at his paper's choice of front-page news. There was no need, we said, to make her private suffering public. It served no greater community interest. It violated her human dignity.

The editor was not receptive. If it will sell papers, he said, I've got the right to use it on the front page. "What makes me sick," he continued, "is when people like you tell me what should be in my paper." He admitted no remorse. He did not admit that we had any valid points. We touched no common ground.

Yet the exchange had meaning. Even though we failed, it was right to stand up for someone who could no longer defend herself. We may have been ineffective in her defense, but it was right to try. We sought to affirm our commitment to her and witness to the worth with which we regarded her.

The woman's two daughters returned home for the service to inter her ashes. During that service we planted a tree behind the church. As the congregation stood around us, these two women sprinkled their mother's ashes over the tree's roots. Then they took earth in their hands, covered the roots, and pressed down the soil to steady the young sapling. These were strong women, and their strength was passed on to me and to those gathered in the sunshine for the service. The two women molded the earth with bare hands, and we were healed and renewed.

I felt related to this family that had suffered. I felt related to the two daughters and their mother. I felt related to the community of friends and family who circled the tree. I felt related to the earth and the forces of life that heal and renew. Here, truly, were things of worth.

Notes

1. David R. Weissbard, *Haggadah for a Unitarian Universalist Seder* (Rockford, IL: The Unitarian Church, 1980).

CHAPTER 5

How Does Evil Happen?

The occasion was a Sunday afternoon gathering of my relatives and friends in the German city where my grandmother had lived as a girl. I was the reason for the occasion—the college student visiting from America. The conversational German sped by—some of it I understood, some I didn't.

There was talk for a while of Muhammad Ali, who had refused to be inducted into the Army. His World Heavyweight title had been taken away. My relatives could not see what one had to do with the other. "He is the best fighter in the world," one young woman said, "He should have the title."

I didn't catch the transition, but then the talk was of the war—World War II. The rise of the Nazis. The Holocaust. And a gulf opened in the room—the family and friends split into two generations, one against the other. Those who had lived through the war were subjected to fierce questioning and censure from those who had come later.

"How could it have happened? This I cannot understand," a woman said. And again, shaking her head, "I cannot understand." One of the older men defended himself, "I, of course, had nothing to do with the Nazis. But the times were hard then. You can't know how difficult it was." The younger group was not mollified. "I am ashamed. I am so ashamed to be German," said one.

The conversation was heated for a while, but finally there wasn't anything left to say. The woman who had spoken for the rights of Muhammad Ali noticed me. When the discussion became heavy, my presence was forgotten, but now I was there again. She said, "You must think we are terrible people."

I didn't think they were terrible people. I thought they were ordinary people caught in currents running faster than they could resist or understand. I did not think they were terrible people, but I didn't know what to say.

How could it have happened? It is the question of evil. Evil is whatever defiles and destroys, robs us of humanity, denies us our potential, brings physical or spiritual death. How does it happen that evil is so present?

Some kinds of evil are understandable: evils resulting from actions taken without full awareness of the consequences, crimes of passion driven by an instant of emotion. All of us have said and done things that we've regretted. We've been propelled by strong feelings into actions that hurt other people. It's not good that this happens, but it is understandable. My faith is not shaken.

There are other kinds of evil that, while bringing tragedy, do not cause me severe theological problems: disease, premature death, the heart attack that fells the good person in the prime of life, the accident that paralyzes, the illness that ends a life too soon. It's terrible when such things happen, but they don't threaten my way of understanding the world. I don't hold to a faith that finds reward or punishment in each event. I do not see judgment in each evil that occurs. Some events just happen arbitrarily, randomly, without cause for blame. They aren't retribution from God. Such evil does not shake my faith.

What does shake me to the core is evil consciously pursued by rational and intelligent individuals who may possess many admirable qualities. Educated and cultured people organized the slaughter in Hitler's Germany. Idealists committed to a new paradise on earth planned the annihilation of their countrymen in Cambodia. People in power in every society put policies into effect knowing that they will hurt fellow travelers on this planet—and then go home to dinner with their families, tuck their children into bed and wish them a safe night. My faith is challenged as I realize that each human being sometimes chooses evil.

How can ordinary human beings—good people, caring people, decent people—choose to hurt others? Why do people of dignity and worth act to deprive others of that same dignity and worth? If, as religious liberals believe, people have the capacity and the desire to choose what is right and true, how can people, instead, choose evil?

I look to the Unitarian Universalist tradition for guidance and find several themes in our efforts to account for evil.

To the nineteenth-century Unitarians, evil resulted from deprivation. The person capable of evil was one whose moral capacity had not been developed or one who had received insufficient education to distinguish right from wrong. Or this was a person whose lack of necessities in life—food and shelter, love and respect—made it impossible to consider moral choice, fairness, or compassion. The Unitarians believed that within each person resides a spark of good, but that spark has to be nourished. Hence, the social reformers of Unitarian conviction devoted efforts toward enabling the deprived to obtain adequate food and shelter. They sought to provide education for those who had been denied it, and they encouraged moral development. They believed that they would address the root causes of evil and therefore weaken its hold upon our life on this earth.

It was a rational understanding of evil that called for a rational response. And the social reformers of liberal religious conviction have made outstanding contributions to easing suffering and removing the causes of evil in this world. But for a rational response to evil to be effective, evil itself must be rational. Often it isn't. Evil is perpetrated by the educated as well as the uneducated, by the prosperous as well as the deprived, by those who have received love and attention as well as those who have been treated as worthless. The Unitarian efforts to understand and respond to evil have foundered when the evil turned out to be not as rational as we.

The essential Universalist affirmation was of a loving God. A loving God, the Universalists believed, would not destine human souls to eternal punishment. Similarly, a loving God would not permit evil in this world if it were not for a purpose. The purpose of evil, according to the nineteenth-century Universalists, was to guide humanity toward good. This could be accomplished, they believed, because the experience of evil is ultimately unpleasant. When we hurt other people, we also feel the hurt and thus are led to be more compassionate. When we defile or desecrate, we too experience defilement and desecration and so are taught to avoid that path.

This affirmation has fueled a long and productive involvement in social concerns. Universalists sought to be agents of a loving God, expressing the care they found in the universe in their everyday interactions with people. They sought to heal human suffering because, they believed, this is what God intends. The Universalists affirmed that all are to be saved, and they guided their lives by that vision.

There was, and is, truth to the Universalist approach to evil. We do learn from our encounter with it, and sometimes we change. But this approach also shows its limits when confronted with radical evil. I may learn a lesson when I mistreat a friend or when I fail to be compassionate to one who is in need. But there is no lesson powerful enough to justify the gas chambers and the firing squads of Nazi Germany. And no greater good can justify the torture of a hostage or the death of an innocent victim. And no positive result can justify the rape of a woman or the abuse of a child. Here is evil beyond the power of even a loving God to turn to good purposes.

The liberal religious responses to evil have made a difference in the world. Unitarians and Universalists have participated in the fight against slavery. They have brought about more humane treatment of the mentally ill. They have established hospitals and schools; they have fought for the rights of minorities; they have engaged in the struggle to free people from poverty. These efforts continue in the struggle for human rights, in the urging of international ties to lessen the danger of war, in responding with compassion and aid for those who suffer. We have urged that people not be resigned to evil but struggle against it and work toward a more humane world. The efforts of Unitarian Universalists have shown significant results, and they continue to do so.

But I also find weaknesses in our approach. We can be slow to recognize radical evil—evil too vast to be understood as a means toward good. We can fail to recognize that evil is perpetrated by people who are not deprived, who enjoy the same benefits that we do, whose spark of good has had every opportunity to develop. We can fail to perceive the evil that we ourselves perpetrate even as we try to bring good into the world. When we encounter such evil, we are unprepared. We may not even recognize it.

Neville Chamberlain, who came from a family long active in British Unitarianism, did what seemed the honorable thing in negotiating with Hitler. He sought to establish trust and take a risk to avoid a war that surely would envelop a continent. When he announced that he had secured, "peace in our time," it was to cheering crowds. But he had missed something crucial. He had not seen the dimension of evil with which he was faced.

And so he lives in history not as one who made a dramatic witness for good but one whose naiveté in the face of evil paved the way toward greater catastrophe.

His crime was that he did not see how this could ever happen.

❖ ❖ ❖

There are times when I have glimpsed the evil that I, myself, can do. One such occasion took place when I was in the fourth grade.

In the fourth grade it was prestigious to wear a Cub Scout uniform—the blue shirt with badges and arrowheads sewed on, the bright yellow scarf. When I wore my Cub Scout uniform, people looked up to me.

On the day my den had its meeting, I wore my Cub Scout uniform to school. Of course, the meeting was right after school—there wasn't time to change. Besides, I wanted to wear my uniform. As I walked down the street, I could feel people stealing glances. I knew they were thinking, "Boy, there goes a Cub Scout."

My neighbor was a Cub Scout too. We both were in the fourth grade, and we walked to school together. One morning I arrived at my friend's house, and when he answered the door I was shocked to see him wearing his Cub Scout uniform. This wasn't the day of his den meeting. It wasn't right. I burned inside as we walked to school.

By the time we reached the playground, I could hold it in no more. I found another boy and pointed to my friend, "Look at this guy. He's wearing his Cub Scout uniform. Who does he think he is?" "Yeah," agreed the boy I had pulled into this, and he issued the challenge, "Who do you think you are?" Then others came, drawn by loud voices, and there grew a wave of taunting and teasing. The boys who joined the commotion had no idea why this boy was receiving such abuse, but they added their voices until he was backed against the wall and in tears.

The mob I had started finally tired of this pursuit and moved on to other things, but I stayed behind, shocked and ashamed at what had taken place. I went to my friend in the Cub Scout uniform to say that I was sorry, but as I spoke he lashed out with both fists, and a teacher had to pull us apart. In his tears and in the force of his blows, I felt his hurt.

I glimpsed evil that morning in my desire to bring him down. I saw it in the crowd of boys who converged upon one of their own when he showed weakness. I didn't think I was an evil person, and I didn't think my classmates were evil, but there was evil on that playground that morning, and it came from within each of us.

How can it happen? Rarely does evil enter this world through self-acknowledged bad people doing bad things. Evil enters this world as ordinary people pursue ordinary dreams and ambitions of life. Evil comes into the world through people who see themselves as good, trying to do good things.

I pursue my goals and my dreams and my values, and that must be good. But sometimes these goals and dreams and values become so strong that I ignore warnings that they may be flawed. I lose track of the human costs as I forge ahead, failing to notice that people I care about deeply may be shoved aside.

I value loyalty. I will serve conscientiously my nation or my religion or an organization whose ideals I support, and surely loyalty cannot be bad. But sometimes loyalty narrows vision. We see the world only in terms of how a particular event affects our own people. We idolize what we are loyal to and thereby miss deeper truths that warn us when those we are loyal to may be wrong.

I am conscientious. I work hard and study hard. I put my best efforts into each project. That must be good; it is a virtue, we often are told, upon which society is built. But extra effort takes time away from something else or someone else. I may ignore people as I pursue my ambition of a job well done. I may neglect myself, and that is not good.

I seek knowledge to understand life, and I seek power to control life. Knowledge and power, in themselves, are not evil. But there is more to existence than what I can understand and control. I become cut off from the wisdom in things I cannot understand, and I fail to pay heed to what I cannot control. Life is wiser than I, but I become too full of my own knowledge and ambitions to notice.

I want to survive, to live a full and healthy life. That certainly is good. Is not survival the evidence for being among the fittest? Not necessarily. The greatest good is achieved by those who have taken risks with their lives, such as Gandhi and Martin Luther King, Jr. Those who play it safe may only perpetuate the status quo. I cling too hard to life, and in that there is evil.

Good and evil are intertwined. Lofty ideals may bring evil consequences. When we are absolutely sure that we are doing good, we then must be especially careful to consider that maybe we are not. Yes, there is inherent human worth and dignity, but it does not follow that everything we do is worthy and dignified. We have not intended evil and so when it happens we are shocked and cry out, "How could this have happened?"

❖ ❖ ❖

We cannot claim to understand evil fully. We will never be able to predict with certainty when benevolent aims will have destructive consequences. We will often be surprised. But there are lessons we can learn.

We learn that the potential for evil is within each person. We each have the capacity to defile life, to demean and destroy and dehumanize. Good and conscientious and hard-working people, and people with strong beliefs and admirable traits can bring suffering and even horror into the world. Worthy aims do not always bring worthy results.

When I forget the potential for evil that I carry with me and that my friends and family also are capable of harm, then I may not suspect that anything wrong can come from our actions. I may not even recognize evil when it appears. One survivor of the Holocaust said, "Why, why did we walk like meek sheep to the slaughterhouse? Why did we not fight back? I know why: because we did not really think that human beings were capable of such crimes."

We also learn that evil festers when we cut ourselves off from each other. In the spaces we create between people grows wariness, suspicion, and perhaps hate. When neighbors keep apart from each other, when people of different religions shut themselves in their own communities, when races refuse to interact, when nations discourage contact with other nations: then we lose awareness of our common humanity, and we forget that our fates are interconnected. We harden ourselves to each other and can ignore the abuse of another. We are not bothered by his or her suffering.

Whenever we are being prepared to do evil to others we hear that they are different from us. They don't value life as we do. Or they won't work like we do. Or they don't believe in God as we do. Or their

God is not the same as ours—their God is the wrong God. When we claim such differences, we view other people as less valuable. It doesn't matter, then, if they're mistreated, persecuted, tortured, removed. For they are not as fully human as we.

We learn too that evil occurs when we cut ourselves off from relationship with the earth. We forget that we are nourished and limited by a common ground of existence. We poison the land; we dump refuse into the waters; we abuse our bodies. We regard ourselves as somehow separate from land and water and other living things. We seek our own enrichment at the expense of the earth, and we become capable of doing great harm—not just to our shared planet but to each other. As Chief Seattle warned,

> You must teach your children that the ground beneath their feet is the ashes of our grandparents. So that they will respect the land, tell your children that the earth is rich with the lives of our kin. Teach your children what we have taught our children— that the earth is our mother. Whatever befalls the earth, befalls the sons [and daughters] of the earth. If [people] spit upon the ground, they spit upon themselves.[1]

We also may cut ourselves off from the force of life. Then we become unwitting agents of evil. We imagine ourselves independent and self-sufficient. We glory in the control we exert over life. We boast of our ability to turn dreams into reality. We become impressed with our own power and intelligence and our ability to work hard to get precisely what we want.

But we fail to take life into account. We become so enamored of our independence that we shield ourselves from the lessons everyday existence teaches us. When we lose the humility that is life's most powerful lesson, we are set to do evil. The stage was set for a war in Vietnam in which the world's most powerful nation was defeated because we lost humility and could not hear warnings that even our power had limits. Or we find societies of utopian dreams that turn so easily to terror because the ideals of the better life do not take people into account. Or we pursue personal ambitions that lead toward self-destruction because we refuse to hear the cautions that life puts before us. We become separated from life, and then it can happen: evil finds its way into our world.

For several summers the Unitarians of Great Britain have brought children from the war-torn city of Belfast, Northern Ireland, to the English countryside. These Catholic and Protestant children in Northern Ireland see each other only as enemies. But for a few weeks during the summer, they live and play together and come to know each other as human beings.

I visited with a couple that served as houseparents one year. They told me of how when the children first arrived, they were tense. At night they roamed the halls, waiting for trouble outside to begin. But this was the English countryside—they were surrounded by farmers and sheep. No trouble came. Only as their time in England was ending did they begin to trust the quiet.

During the first days these children divided into Catholics and Protestants as was their custom. The housemother overheard a discussion among several Protestant boys about body parts. When they came to sexual organs, one said, "Oh, Catholics don't have those." The group apparently accepted that as a truth, and the conversation moved on.

As their time together continued, the Catholic and Protestant groups broke up, and children began to be together as children. I would guess they discovered that both Catholics and Protestants "have those." But that snippet of conversation conveyed a chilling idea—a child's interpretation of what he had been told: that those on the other side are different. So different as to be of another species. So different as to be not human.

When we become so separate from each other that we forget our common humanity, then evil certainly can happen. When we no longer feel compassion for a human being who is suffering, when we pursue our goals with such fervor that we do not perceive their human effects, when we care only for those of our own kind, then evil has made its way into the world. When we grow apart from each other, we separate ourselves from life. In that is evil.

❖ ❖ ❖

What guidance can religious liberalism offer in my search for a response to evil? We do not possess a doctrine of the final nature of evil. We cannot promise that someday evil will be banished. We do not foresee a final battle between the forces of good and evil but find this battle going on within each person every day. How do we decrease the power of evil and promote good?

For me, the starting point is to establish relationship. I resist evil by trying to overcome the separateness that keeps us apart from each other, from the earth, and from life.

I try to bring people together whose understandings of life may differ, whose perspectives may clash, people who often are separated by barriers of class or race or culture. Unitarian Universalist congregations include people of different religious backgrounds. We come together and form religious communities in which we can be together and respect diversity. We try also to reach out from our congregations so that we may work together, understand each other, appreciate each other. In bridging the gaps that keep us apart, we make it less likely that we will do evil to each other.

In our religious education programs, the youngest children are taught about forming relationships. They are introduced to adults in the congregations and encouraged to get to know grown-ups who are not part of their immediate family. As they grow older, children are taught about peoples different from themselves—the religion of a child in Africa, the everyday life of a child in Latin America. And as they reach teenage years, their classes may meet with teenagers from other religious communities so that they understand people with other perspectives and appreciate them and care about them. Several Unitarian Universalist congregations have adopted refugee families from war-torn areas of the world. What happens to these people becomes our own concern, not just an item on the news. Adults in the congregation help the families get settled. The congregation's children also provide assistance. Through the experience we are related to a wider experience of humanity, and we are changed.

The Unitarian Universalist involvement in social concerns starts with the assumption of our relatedness to the peoples of the earth. We are not separate from those who suffer. Those who are poor and exploited are not different from us.

A Unitarian Universalist minister tells of how he came to understand the plight of the poor in Latin America—to feel related to the poor throughout the world. He was in Mexico City and was shown a dump where 5,000 people lived.

Shortly after we pulled into the dump and began to drive

slowly through I saw a little girl who was about ten years old carrying a huge plastic bag of cans and bottles slung over her shoulder and weighing her down like the cross of Christ. Her eyes remained fixed on the ground in front of her. She was barefoot. Her face was without expression. I looked at her as intensely as I could and watched from the back window of the van even after we passed. Sharp pain pierced my heart.

The image of that little girl has stayed with me and it haunts me. When I hear about poor people I think of her. It's uncomfortable. Poor people are more easily talked about from a philosophical point of view when they are at a safe distance, not when they are so real.

Frank Hall
The Unitarian Church
Westport, Connecticut

The memory of that little girl is painful. The realization of relationship opens us to her suffering. But it also may spur us to become involved and confront the evils in the world.

Our involvement may take the form of helping a person who is in need: one who volunteers to read for a person who is blind, another who makes himself or herself available to do repairs and chores for an older person living alone, still another who shops for a person who cannot get out of the house. Or involvement may take the form of influencing legislation, lobbying, applying political pressure so that those who are weak and in need will not be ignored. Or the involvement may be making a public witness as did Unitarian Universalists who marched for civil rights in Selma or as have those who have demonstrated against the escalating arms race. Our responses to evil may be different, but they are centered in a sense of relationship. We share in this life, and from that image of unity comes our mission and hope.

To seek relationship is a simple aim but not so easy to live. Through seeking relationship we may expose ourselves to risk, and we may sometimes make mistakes. Often we will feel awkward and vulnerable. But evil is less likely to control someone who lives with openness to his or her brothers and sisters. And we are less likely to be led by a narrow and destructive vision into actions that do violence to those with whom we share this earth.

How could it have happened? How were good people, educated people, caring people converted to the Nazi cause? How do ordinary and decent people become agents of evil?

My relatives in Germany are good people, devoted to their children and families, loyal friends. Germany is a nation of good people. How could it have happened?

It happens when people forget that we all are part of the same human family. It happens when Christians see themselves as essentially different from Jews, Protestants from Catholics, Muslims from Christians. It happens when capitalists see themselves as essentially different from communists, whites from blacks, people of Western society from people of Eastern society, men from women. When we separate humanity into warring camps, evil can appear.

It happens when we cut ourselves off from the suffering of others and do not get involved. "I had nothing to do with the Nazis," proclaimed my uncle as if that absolved him from responsibility. But it didn't. For when we simply "have nothing to do with" evil, then we allow it to be. We are responsible. We are part of the same family of humanity. We share the same earth, the same force of life.

"The basic sin," Gandhi observed, "the only sin in the ultimate analysis, is the sin of separateness."[2]

Notes

1. Chief Seattle, as quoted in Tirrell H. Kimball, *Honoring Our Mother Earth* (Portland, Maine: Allen Avenue Unitarian Universalist Church, 1988), p. 13.

2. Mohandas Gandhi, as quoted in Mathew Fox, *Original Blessing* (Sante Fe: Bear & Co., 1983), p. 49.

CHAPTER 6

How Shall I Live?

H ow shall I live? It is the question of ethics. How may my beliefs be expressed in action? What implications do my religious affirmations have for the life I lead?

The question of how we live is particularly important in the liberal religious tradition. It marks another significant difference with orthodoxy, where one is saved by belief, not deeds. In orthodox teaching, the kindest and most benevolent person will not find salvation if his or her doctrine is in error. If one questions too freely or does not accept key teachings of the church, then it doesn't matter how good a life a person leads, one still is not saved.

This view takes a matter of speculation—religious doctrine—and elevates it to a place of authority higher than the observed deeds of people. It favors a person of orthodox beliefs, whether or not he or she contributes to human life. It disdains the person who makes great contributions but who questions orthodox doctrine. In addition, the resources of the religious community are used more to establish and enforce belief than to try to make a difference in this world.

As a child I heard the orthodox minister pound the pulpit in censorship of "other" religions. I looked into the faces around me, but they revealed no complaint. From that day I stopped idealizing the minister. I began to notice the narrow and exclusive attitudes held by the parishioners. My twelve-year-old mind rebelled at the blind following of tradition. I wanted answers to my questions, but my fellows accused me of being a heretic.

Soon I was visiting other denominations but never stayed for long. The folks in the church and tents were able to believe in dogma, and I could not. I desperately needed to belong somewhere, but I felt uncomfortable with each viewpoint. So for many years I wandered in the wilderness of disenchantment and found no anchor in my sea of questions about life's purpose.

Some deep longing made me continually take informal classes in comparative philosophies. I noticed that a core of the same faces attended, and I found their questions echoed my own. One day, while the TV news told another story about man's inhumanity to man, I became outraged. My eyes flowed with tears, and I wailed to no one in particular, "Why does this happen? What can I do to help relieve the world's pain?"

A brilliant light seemed to have gone down my spine and engulfed me. An inner dam seemed to have opened and into my thoughts poured new answers to old questions. With eyelashes rainbowy wet with tears, I followed an inner edict to dial the operator and ask for numbers of organizations which promote community well being between races and creeds. On the wave of this exhilarated feeling, I dialed and made an appointment with a local agency. I began then a lifelong career of volunteering my meager talents to service organizations.

It was not long before I saw the same people in these groups whom I had seen at the comparative philosophy studies. When I asked them where they went to church, I was invited to visit the Unitarian Universalists. At last I found a religious body I could respect and follow. Within this congregation I enjoy full fellowship at last.

> *Viola M. Henne*
> *Michael Servetus Unitarian Fellowship*
> *Vancouver, Washington*

In orthodoxy, God is omnipotent. God alone grants salvation. If God could be swayed by acts of human beings—no matter how noteworthy—then He no longer would be in full control. In this view, God's power would be compromised if He were influenced by the good deeds of human beings. Hence, God chooses those who are saved for His own reasons—reasons that must remain inscrutable to humans. Salvation is not a result of what one does in life but comes through being chosen by God. The appropriate human response is not to work hard in order to be picked by God. It is, rather, to have faith and to live with the assurance that such faith brings.

Religious liberals have never been able to accept this argument. To us, it cheapens life on this earth. It values what we actually do with our lives less than our statements of belief. This view also promotes a concept of God that few of us can accept. For the orthodox, God is a ruler whose primary attribute is power. But if we view God as a creative force, as an interdependent web of existence, then power is not the main characteristic. Submission is not our primary response. Rather, God calls mortals to work with life's creative forces to shape a society based in care, justice, and compassion. The building of a just and compassionate society is not just God's project but is a responsibility shared by human beings. Hence, good works count.

There are many implications to this difference between the liberal and orthodox positions.

For the orthodox, an atheist is a threat—an individual to be disdained. For the religious liberal, an atheist is respected and affirmed if he or she lives honestly and makes a positive contribution to life. We value the atheist who lives with integrity as highly as the person of orthodox convictions who lives with integrity.

For the orthodox, conversion is a central experience—accepting the truth of doctrine or the truth of Christ. To the religious liberal, the emphasis upon conversion is misplaced. We ask, so what if the person is converted? The real question is how this individual lives. If the new faith helps the person to face life with courage and hope, then the conversion is to be celebrated. But if the experience of conversion is simply a "high" that has no effect on the individual's deeds, then it is hard to find much of significance about the event.

Orthodox tenets can be used to justify the persecution and punishment of those who do not share their beliefs. Time and time again throughout the history of religion, belief has been given precedence over life. People are pursued, persecuted, captured, tortured, and killed for no other crime than their honest questioning of doctrine.

When the question, "What do you believe?" becomes more important than the question, "How do you live?" then the way is cleared for considerable mischief and harm.

Unitarian Universalists are especially sensitive to persecution based in religious doctrine because people in our tradition have been victims of those who tried to enforce belief by fire.

Michael Servetus (1511-1553) was a Spanish physician among those credited with discovering that blood circulates through the body. His real passion, however, was theology. He became a student of the Bible and came to convictions later expressed in Unitarian churches. He established no church, but shared his beliefs through his writings. Michael Servetus paid for his beliefs with his life.

It was the Reformation, a period of theological dispute and up-heaval. Martin Luther had brought about the split in the Catholic Church which created Protestantism. John Calvin had established himself at Geneva, Switzerland, where he undertook his life's work of systematizing Protestant thought. Both men were alive when Michael Servetus came upon the scene.

Luther and Calvin asserted that the Bible was the primary source of religious authority. They sought freedom from the hierarchy of the Catholic Church and urged that instead people turn to the Bible for truth and guidance. In his own studies of the Bible, Servetus drew conclusions not shared by the Protestant or Catholic leadership. He found the Jesus of the New Testament markedly different from the Christ of doctrine. And he found little justification in the Bible for a central teaching of all Christianity—the doctrine of the trinity.

In his book, *On the Errors of the Trinity,* Servetus argued that the doctrine of the trinity is not supported in the Bible. The idea of the trinity is that God is three: Father, Son, and Holy Spirit. An implication of this teaching is that Jesus is regarded as God—part of the Trinity of Father, Son, Holy Spirit. Servetus claimed that the Biblical scriptures do not support this formula—it is a creation of doctrine. Jesus is not God. God is not three, but one. Servetus was labeled an "anti-trinitarian." But from his position comes the term "unitarian" meaning "God is one."

When Servetus's book appeared, it was denounced by the Protes-tant leadership. The Reformation had been a radical step. Its leaders were not ready to take a still more radical step of questioning a teaching so central to Christianity as the trinity and hence the divinity of Christ. And so word went out to capture Servetus and bring him to justice. He escaped to France, where for twenty years he lived under an assumed name. He practiced medicine, served as an editor, and lectured at the University of Paris.

But theology remained the passion of Michael Servetus. He could not keep himself from studying the Bible and sharing his ideas. After twenty years he published a second book, *The Restoration of Christianity*. Servetus argued that people should turn away from selfishness to sacrifice and devote themselves to a life of love and service. How should we live? According to Servetus, we should emulate Christ. He also stated that only after a person is old enough to make an informed decision should he or she choose to be baptized as a Christian.

This proposal was another slap at the new Protestant hierarchy. Not only had Servetus challenged the doctrine of the trinity, he now advocated adult baptism. To add insult to injury, Servetus had come to such teachings by doing what the Protestant leaders were advocating—by studying the Bible.

Servetus was imprisoned by the French Inquisition, but he escaped. He tried to flee to Naples, but his route took him through John Calvin's Geneva, where he was recognized and captured. Over the years, he had written to Calvin challenging him and offering to instruct him on the errors of his teachings. Calvin had grown to detest Servetus and he made sure that Servetus would never leave Geneva alive. Servetus was charged with heresy and burned at the stake, with a copy of his book tied to his arm. Protestants and Catholics scoured the countryside for other copies of the book and burned each one they could find.[1]

The execution of Michael Servetus engendered considerable criticism of John Calvin. At issue was whether mortal human beings have the right to execute other mortal human beings because of differences of religious belief. Calvin stated that heresy was a more terrible crime than murder and should be punished accordingly. But now other voices were raised. Sebastian Castellio (1515-1563) spoke out against the treatment of Servetus. "To kill a man is not to protect a doctrine," he wrote, "but it is to kill a man. When the Genevans killed Servetus, they did not defend a doctrine, but they killed a man."[2]

If a person questions the doctrine established by church authorities, is that a more terrible crime than murder? Is belief so much more important than ethics that murder can be justified in the name of enforcing belief? What kind of belief allows human beings to torture others in the name of truth and right? If Christ were to return to earth, would not He, too, be branded a heretic and burned for questioning doctrine?

When churches later were formed and took the name Unitarian, tolerance was a central value. They would not persecute others who differed with their beliefs. They would be open to differences. Their focus would not be upon intricacies of belief but upon how people would live. Rather than worshipping Jesus as a God, they would regard him as a teacher. As Jesus urged compassion and charity and forgiveness, they too would try to live with compassion and charity and forgiveness.

For these new churches, issues of ethics were primary. They preached what some have called practical Christianity as their teachings focused upon the everyday implications of religion. Questions of belief remained important, but the real test of a person was how he or she lived. And the test of a religious community was how the people of that faith conduct their lives and treat their neighbors. A faith that brings suffering to human beings in the name of truth cannot be a worthy faith.

❖ ❖ ❖

How shall I live? Generations of Unitarians and Universalists have responded to this question. We have sought to live ethically in this world.

The Universalist Clara Barton taught school for fifteen years. She noticed that poor children did not have access to education and so she pioneered a free school. During the Civil War she cared for the wounded—though she had been told that the battlefield was no place for a woman—and used supplies donated by Universalist churches. Later, she went to Europe and discovered the Red Cross. She brought the idea to the United States and established the American Red Cross. In so doing Clara Barton lived the Universalist teaching that we all are saved. Her work with schools affirmed that the poor as well as the wealthy have rights to education. And she demonstrated that those who are in need—from war or disaster or personal crisis—deserve our compassion and care.[3]

The Unitarian Jane Addams was born with a crooked spine, and she walked pigeon-toed. As a child she was subject to the taunts of her classmates. She never forgot the feeling of unfairness and

injustice that welled up in her as she was being teased. She determined to devote her life to fighting injustice wherever she found it.
The opportunity presented itself when she bought a house in the
middle of Chicago and founded Hull House. There children of poor
families had the opportunity to play and be educated, and children of
immigrants could learn English. Hull House served the poor, and it
became a center for activities aimed at social reform. Jane Addams
became known all over the world as a person who made a difference.
She was called "The American Saint."[4]

John Haynes Holmes was a Unitarian minister serving The Community Church in New York City. He had a vision of a church not
simply as a community for spiritual search and nourishment but also
as a place from which action could proceed. He had a vision of a
church that would bring together people of different backgrounds:
race, creed, nationality, class. He envisioned a church in which
people would commit themselves to addressing the injustices of
society. John Haynes Holmes sought to live by his own vision. In
1909 he helped organize the NAACP. He supported Margaret Sanger
and the Planned Parenthood movement. He worked against poverty,
fought for civil liberties, and was an outspoken pacifist. He made a
difference.[5]

I look also to the example of current members of Unitarian
Universalist congregations. How do we express the values of our
religious tradition in our decisions and actions?

My first pregnancy ended in miscarriage at sixteen weeks. It
was a time of much pain—both physical and emotional. During
the days I spent recovering at home, I received several phone
calls, two of which touched me deeply. They, together with a
third incident, changed forever how I respond to others in pain.

One call was from a casual friend. After the initial greetings
she said, "Do you want to talk about it?" And talk I did—for an
hour—finally getting in touch with all those feelings I'd hidden:
the pain, despair and anger. This was the beginning of my
period of mourning and also of a close and treasured friendship.

The second call came from a woman with whom I'd taught.
She said, "I just wanted to tell you that I really don't know what
to say to you at a time like this, but I want you to know that I'm
thinking about you." I was so moved by her ability to put her

own discomfort aside to let me know that she recognized my pain.

Upon my return to work, most of my colleagues welcomed me back or asked how I was feeling. One man in my department said, "Welcome back. I was so sorry to hear about the baby." I almost kissed him. Someone acknowledged that I hadn't been out with the flu for a week!

So, how shall I live my life? I shall try to acknowledge the pain of others and, when appropriate, be there to listen to it.

Pat Maravel
Unitarian Universalist Fellowship
Huntington, New York

In my line of work—carpentry, home improvement, general contracting—I often find myself working with people who view those of different ethnic, racial, sexual or national characteristics as inferior to them. I cannot count the number of times I have heard the word "nigger" used, been told a "Polack" joke, or been informed of the inadequacies of women except, of course, as sexual objects.

For a long time I remained silent. Slowly, I began to reveal my dissatisfaction with such references. At first, my objections were treated lightly, jokingly. But gradually my co-workers learned that, at least when I was around, such references were to be eliminated. I maintained a sense of humor about myself so as not to appear shrill, but I held my ground.

One of the great moments in my life came when one of my former partners, one I had given up on a long time ago as being so bigoted that he was beyond hope, informed me that, as a result of my persistent commitment to tolerance and understanding, he had actually begun to look at minority groups less stereotypically. That one small affirmation has meant more to me than all the years of experiences I have had with like-minded people in my peace, youth, and church groups.

To live my life affirming tolerance, justice, and love among those who don't share these values and to affect a change of heart, no matter how small, is a truly rewarding experience.

Patrick Fleeharty
Unitarian Universalist Church
Anne Arundel County, Maryland

I was a believer in the rightness of the Korean War. My history teacher in high school in 1947 in a special segment on the United Nations had given me a great respect for the purposes of that body. I accepted the idea that the war was essentially about an immoral aggressor nation being prevented by a principled United Nations from reaching its objectives. I was prepared to do my duty for a good cause....

[This new soldier soon found himself on the front line in Korea commanding a tank, even though back home in Kentucky, he had not yet learned to drive a car.]

The tanks of our company were used as pill boxes along a ridge overlooking the valley that separated us from North Korean troops. As a tank commander I did my job responsibly. I made sure the other crew members kept things in working order and that they tended to serious business. I manned the gun often during the daylight hours. It took usually only two rounds to destroy the target, mostly a construction of sandbags, which appeared daily. I was in constant touch by an intercom system with the artillery forward observer, who had an even more powerful scope and he helped me spot things I might have missed. One day he reported that he had spotted an enemy soldier lying on the crest of the hill facing us. Without thinking I jumped into the tank and fired a round in the direction he was indicating. I had assumed that when the first round had landed the man would run for cover.

Instead, the observer announced that I had scored a direct hit, on the first shot, miraculously. The first official Killed in Action was called into headquarters on my behalf and I got a cheery congratulation from everyone on the hill. But I felt terrible.

Up to that moment I had just been trying to do the best job I could, the same as I did as an athlete, a college student, a trainee. For the first time I realized that excellence in performance was in conflict with more deeply felt beliefs. All I could think of for days was that single official Killed in Action whom I never saw. For many days I lived in a kind of limbo. As far as I could tell, I still believed in the military mission and felt my role was a proper one. I was in mental conflict, but I carried on my duties as before. I was sleep-walking toward a moment of truth.

One day I got a call from the artillery forward observer telling me that an enemy soldier was standing in plain sight on one of the hills opposite us. I found him in my scope, as clear as if he were standing no more than a hundred yards from me. I stared at him, unbelieving, angry that he was so careless. He looked like a man who had just gone up there for a breath of fresh air, certainly not a sly enemy bent on my destruction.

The observer was shouting to fire, for God's sake, for he will get away. I simply said to him, "I'm not going to do it." I wasn't going to drop a 35mm shell on another human being, even if he were an enemy soldier. The next moment I was brought up short by the voice of my company commander, who was hooked up to the intercoms of all tanks. "I order you to fire at that man," he said. "Yes sir," I answered instinctively and just as quickly adjusted my gun so that I would miss the man by a great distance. The company commander said he would be visiting me the next day. I had all night to think what I was going to say to him.

I had no experience as a rebel. I was never one to seek responsibility, but whatever responsibility I was given I accepted. I considered the possibility of characterizing my behavior as an aberration and assuring him it wouldn't happen again, but I knew I would only be delaying an inevitable crisis. I knew that at this moment in my life I had either to say to this man, "I am through killing people," or feel corrupted for the rest of my life. How could I justify this decision? I was not raised in any religious tradition that ruled out the taking of life in these circumstances. I was simply a free thinker, a person they would see as having the least right to object to the taking of life. Was I simply being immature? Was I avoiding life's most difficult requirements? Did I lack courage? And what of my conviction that the United Nations troops were doing an important service? If I really held that belief, wasn't killing the necessary, albeit ugly, consequence?

These questions, doubts, and attempts at reasoning and justification churned in my mind most of the night. But the only thing I could really cling to in the end was the simple thought,

"I am not going to kill anybody anymore." I felt my life would rise or fall with that declaration.

The next morning he came: tall, lean, grim, weathered, dressed in green fatigues with helmet and flak jacket, double bars on the collar. We wasted no time in pleasantries. He spoke in low tones, more perplexed and impatient than angry, and gave plenty of room for me to make my case.

Standing on that dirt road that undulated along our defense line, separated only by hillside bunkers from no-man's land and the enemy, we debated issues of war and peace, death, beliefs, and humanity's greatest loyalties. He suggested my problem may have stemmed from shooting at people from inside the protective armor of the tank. To some extent I believe he was correct about that, but I insisted it was a matter of reverence of life, not of concern for a fair fight. He suggested I would feel differently if I had seen the mutilated bodies of our men, some of whom had fallen right where we were standing a few days before I had come on line. I said I could feel no anger at the men who fired those killing rounds, for they were doing no worse than I. He asked me if I did not love my country and want to fight for it. I answered that it was patriotic fervor that was causing the prolonging aggression of one people against another.

Finally, after a silence, he said, "Well, it's up to you." I said, "No, it's up to you. I am not going to kill any more human beings." He said, "Pack your things." After two weeks in limbo, I was transferred to the military police....

[Some thirty years after his moment of decision on a battlefield in Korea, this Unitarian Universalist reports,]

I have always been proud of my act. I felt I was finding out for the first time who I really was. I felt that in life I was going to be a careful voyager, valuing my own life, taking no unnecessary risks. No hero, certainly. But I felt that when issues arose, issues of right and wrong, life and death, joy and anguish, I was going to put my life or wealth on the line and let fate do what it will. That feeling gave me enormous strength.

Bruce Gordon
First Parish
Lexington, Massachusetts

It is a fundamental principle of the Unitarian Universalist tradition that how we live is the most important test of our beliefs. That principle guides us in our everyday interactions with each other as it urges us to play a role in nudging society toward greater justice and opportunity and compassion.

❖ ❖ ❖

How shall I live? By seeking to be faithful to my religious affirmations in the choices and deeds of everyday life: respect for people, compassion for those who suffer, openness toward those who differ with me, justice for those who are treated unfairly, affirmation of the right of conscience.

A belief that underlies the Unitarian Universalist emphasis upon ethics is that we *can* make a difference. We need not be resigned to the status quo, and we ought not let ourselves become cynical. We can become engaged in the struggles of existence, and we can influence each other's lives and the shape of human society.

It changes us to assert that we do not have to accept the world as we find it; it changes us to believe that through our efforts we can make a difference. For then we take responsibility for our own lives and for that offered by our society.

I do not always succeed in being faithful to my beliefs. Often my expectations are greater than what I can achieve. Sometimes I feel overwhelmed by the magnitude of the challenges and discouraged by the slow pace of reform. Occasionally, I am tempted to give up.

But at these times I return to the affirmation for which people in our tradition have lived and sometimes died: it matters how we live. We have the power to prod our society toward greater justice and compassion, and we have the power to make a difference in each other's lives.

Notes

1. Roland Bainton, *Hunted Heretic* (Boston: Beacon Press, 1953); David Parke, *The Epic of Unitarianism* (Boston: Beacon Press, 1957), pp. 1-7; Willard C. Frank, Jr., *A Year with Our Liberal Heritage* (Tulsa: Unitarian Universalist Advance, 1984), p. 43.

2. Quoted in Earl Morse Wilbur, *A History of Unitarianism: Socianism and its Antecedents* (Boston: Beacon Press, 1945), p. 203.

3. D. Tracy, *A Stream of Living Souls* (Oak Park, IL: Delphi Resources, 1986), pp. 12-15.

4. Ibid, pp. 5-8.

5. Ibid, pp. 38-40.

CHAPTER 7

How Can I Live With Death?

Each of us confronts death. We wonder: How can I go on when someone I care about dies? How can I live, knowing that I too will die? How can I affirm life, realizing that death extinguishes each being?

Each of us dies; the earth, itself, is mortal. This knowledge destroys the illusion of permanence. It reaches into our dreams and shatters our complacency. I wonder how I can invest energy and hope into life, knowing that all I work for and all I care about someday will be no more.

Norbert Capek was a Unitarian minister who served congregations in his native Czechoslovakia. He was devoted to both liberal religion and the cause of self-determination for the Czechoslovak peoples. In facing death at the hands of the Nazis during World War II, he affirmed life as he affirmed his faith.

He was born in 1870, the son of a tailor. The Capek family was Roman Catholic, but interwoven with the Catholic religion was a fierce pride in the Czech people. While Norbert was growing up, Czechoslovakia was part of the Austro-Hungarian empire, but the tales he heard as a boy recalled earlier days of Czech independence. They retold the stories of Czech heros such as Jan Hus, who witnessed to the ideal of a faith that recognized the people's right to choose.

The young Norbert Capek was drawn to religious studies, and he was inspired by the leaders of the Czech church who kept alive the ideal of Czech self-governance. He became involved in the church, beginning the study of religion and assisting the local parish priest.

When he reached high-school age, Norbert went to Vienna to live with his uncle, who hoped Norbert would take over his tailoring business. But the young man's interest in the church got in the way. A friend invited him to Baptist services, and there he was enthralled by the minister's sermons and the topics he addressed. This contrasted with the ritual of the Catholic Church, and Norbert decided that in this faith he could be free to pursue his own interests and convictions. He joined the Baptist church, began to study for the ministry, and left behind the family craft of tailoring.

Capek served Baptist churches with distinction. He was minister of congregations in Bratislava and Hamburg, and founded seven new churches. Soon he was appointed Superintendent of the Baptist churches of Austro-Hungary. But his mind was active and restless, and his faith continued to develop. Despite his success in the Baptist church, his convictions took him beyond its beliefs. When he met the Unitarian Thomas Masaryk—who later became the first president of an independent Czechoslovakia, Capek was ready to transfer his allegiance to Unitarianism.

He planned to establish new Unitarian churches in his native Czechoslovakia, but World War I intervened. Capek was known as an independent and free-thinking leader and so under the threat of imprisonment by Austrian authorities, he came to the United States. Arriving in New York, Capek sought to support his family by serving as minister to Slovakian churches. But he was regarded as too liberal and so he turned to journalism, editing a Czech newspaper in Newark, New Jersey, and writing on Czechoslovakian issues for national newspapers.

While living in East Orange, New Jersey, the Capek family established contact with American Unitarianism. They joined the Unitarian Church in East Orange, which nourished Capek's dream of establishing Czech Unitarian churches. When World War I ended, Capek went to Prague, where he founded a religious society called the Free Religious Fellowship.

This congregation began with forty people, but under Capek's leadership it grew to one of the largest churches in Prague, with more than 5,000 members. In five other cities, liberal congregations were also founded under the leadership and example of Norbert Capek and the Prague Free Religious Fellowship. They espoused a free faith emphasizing reason, tolerance, and human values. It also took on a particularly Czech character, identifying itself with the ideal of Czech independence and self-determination. Capek's personal stamp on the faith came through the music—he composed some 250 hymns for use in the services of the Free Religious Fellowship.

But again war intervened—World War II and the rise of the Nazis, the division of the newly independent Czechoslovakia, and Germany's annexation of Czech regions of the country. In the spring of 1941, Capek was arrested as a threat to Nazism, and imprisoned at Dachau concentration camp. In the face of death, Capek sought to fortify the spirit of his fellow prisoners. Survivors of the camp tell of his patient counsel and of his composing songs, which they sang at the top of their lungs while marching around the barbed-wire enclosure. It was a Yes to life in the midst of death. Through his own courage and example, Capek helped keep alive a burning hope that enabled others to survive.

The concentration camp authorities realized the effect that Capek's presence had on the prisoners, and removed him from contact with them. He was transferred to the "medical experimentation" section, where he died on October 30, 1942.[1]

We remember Norbert Capek for his affirmation of life in the face of death, for his devotion to the Czechoslovak people, for the music he composed, and for his enthusiastic affirmation of a liberal faith. These qualities are expressed in a service that he created for the Free Religious Fellowship and which many Unitarian Universalist congregations observe today, a flower communion service.

It was developed during the early years of the Free Religious Fellowship as a way of expressing the faith which joined this congregation. Each person brought a flower to the service, for the Czechs love flowers. These were placed in a single vase to signify that each individual joined the Fellowship by his or her own choice. All the flowers gathered in the vase symbolized the community—a diverse congregation of people who came together freely.

The gathering of flowers representing a congregation is an affirmation of life. It also is a response to death. Flowers are temporary and mortal. Their beauty, however, is not diminished by their fragility. Indeed, we value a flower because it does not last forever. Each individual flower is temporary, yet new flowers continually grow and bloom, testimony to the force of life that permeates the world. In each new and temporary and mortal flower is an expression of this life force, a Yes to life.

At the end of the flower communion service, each person returns to the vase and takes a flower—but not the one he or she had brought. The people arrive at the service with a flower and leave with another flower—the gift of another person.

The ceremony is an affirmation that despite the death to which both flowers and human beings are subject, there also is a force of life that pulses through our world, renewing and transforming, offering us the diverse gifts of existence. Death does not overcome life. It does not cancel life's meaning. Even in a concentration camp, flowers bloom and people sing. Life renews and transforms. One can say Yes.

❖ ❖ ❖

The condition of life is that those who live also will die. How can I, drawing upon the affirmations of the Unitarian Universalist tradition, respond to the challenge of death?

The focus of our faith is on this world—on the pain and the possibilities of being human. Some Unitarian Universalists believe that individual consciousness survives the death of the body. Others view death as the end of the person and the extinguishing of personality. Yet many Unitarian Universalists regard life after death as an issue too speculative to form the foundations of a faith. Our hope, then, is not centered in a conviction that individual life continues after death. Rather, we seek the implications death has for life.

For me, the starting point is to affirm life. It is the Yes to existence that Norbert Capek proclaimed in the concentration camp. It is the Yes visible in each flower as it blooms during its time on earth, the Yes expressed when we gather in memory of one who has died, the Yes demonstrated whenever a person offers his or her caring to one who has suffered loss. It is the Yes that is our most powerful defiance of that which would defile and demean. Yes, it is a world of death but, Yes, it is also a world of life.

This Yes urges us to participate in life—to commit ourselves fully to the challenges of existence. There is danger and risk in our lives. Death always is a possibility. The lesson is to take what time we have and to live it as well as we can. "Life is no brief candle to me," wrote George Bernard Shaw. "It is a sort of splendid torch which I've got a hold of for a moment, and I want to make it burn as brightly as possible before handing it on to further generations."

This Yes urges us to be compassionate to those who share this temporary life with us. It calls us to respond to the pain of other people. The temptation is to ignore the bonds that join us—to claim independence of humanity and its failings and vulnerability. But death challenges our independence and reminds us that we share in a common existence. In response we seek to be present for the person whose life has been challenged by death.

She died as silently as she was born. We never heard her voice. She never saw us.

I've heard that when a parent dies, you lose a part of your past; when a child dies, you lose part of your future. My husband and I were left with a void in our future. We had lost the "American Dream" that we were living in. We took for granted our good marriage, our modest home, our one child and the one we had planned to have in the future.

When the dream shattered, we found that each of us needed different ways of coping with our grief. My husband's life had not changed as dramatically as mine had. Whether or not our daughter had lived, he would still be going to work each day. I was at home during the day in a house filled with a deafening silence where there should have been a baby's cry. My other daughter was only two-and-a-half and could not be expected to understand why Mommy was sad and short-tempered sometimes. I felt she deserved an interested Mommy, and I had to save up my grief for the end of the day, after she was asleep, to try and work through my feelings.

In a time of such profound grief, one's family cannot always extend the aid needed because they are also grieving. But by being cared for so unselfishly by the greater community of the Unitarian Society of New Haven, our grief was a little easier to bear.

When our second daughter lay in limbo in the hospital, it was our minister who gave us open and honest counsel. When our daughter died, he helped us prepare a loving and moving memorial service. There were many people at the service whom we had never even met. The offers of help and cards and letters received from the congregation certainly helped in the weeks following her death. We felt that we were part of a large family who cared for us.

Our lives have changed in many ways since that sad time. Although statistics say that only one out of seven marriages survive the death of a child, ours has taken on new dimensions. We no longer take life for granted. It sounds melodramatic to say this, but we are grateful just to be alive. We can look beyond the minor annoyances of day to day living and see things in a larger frame.

We are more sensitive to the pain of others and try to reach out to those who need us. We found out how important it is to really listen to people. Those who were willing to sit with us as we went over and over the details of our sorrow did us the most good, and we try to be there for others with a similar need. In addition my husband and I take time to really listen to each other as well. We are no longer afraid of making each other uncomfortable by bringing up unpleasant issues for discussion.

We have managed to rebuild a shattered life with the help of family and friends. Some of these friends we had never even met before the tragedy, but they are among the most important friends—those we met at the Unitarian Society of New Haven.

Linda Freedman
Unitarian Society
New Haven, Connecticut

This is a Yes that also stems from recognizing life's wonder and mystery: a recognition that emerges most powerfully in response to death. A man who has lived with cancer for twenty years writes of his experience,

Although objectivity and pure reason were once for me the foundations of religious truth and value, I now find religious truth to be . . . unfathomable. The ways of God are a mystery to me. No religious theory adequately explains why I contracted cancer; nor do I know why I am alive and not dead. And I have stopped seeking explanations. . . . My faith now is rooted in an experience of receiving daily life as a sheer gift.[2]

And this Yes calls us to respond with gratitude for life. The reality of death asserts that message most powerfully: we need not be here.

In *Generation to Generation,* Tom Owen-Towle observes in a letter to his children,

> None of us asks to be born. There is no personal merit involved with our arrivals. We creatures didn't earn the privilege of life. We were lucky. Whether you look at human existence scientifically or religiously, it is an unspeakable miracle, a wonder, a gift of grace.

We do not have to be alive. Our being alive at this moment is a wonder to which we respond with thanks. As Rabbi Abraham Heschel observed, "Just to be is a blessing. Just to live is holy."

For me an approach to death begins with an affirmation of life. That Yes carries many implications.

In response to the death of one we care about: Say Yes to life. Affirm that person's being. Recognize what he or she lived for. Celebrate the individual. Remember him or her with respect and with love.

In recognition of one's own death: affirm life by participating to the fullest in its joys and challenges and even its sorrows. Say Yes to life by using whatever talents and opportunities we have to contribute to a better community and a better world.

In response to living a mortal life in a mortal world: affirm life. Even though each being dies, a force of life continues, expressing itself in new ways and presenting new possibilities. Live with respect for that life force and care for the many forms through which it is present.

How do I, as a Unitarian Universalist, respond to death? I try to live with gratitude that comes from recognizing that my life is temporary—not to be taken for granted. And I am guided by reverence for the gift of life that each of us shares, tasting both the joys and the pain of existence.

❖ ❖ ❖

Unitarian Universalist memorial observances express this approach to life and death.

We had a beloved neighbor who was stricken with cancer. She suffered a long time before she died. We were invited to the

funeral service at the Unitarian Church in Toronto. Our friend
had never been a churchgoer, but the Unitarian minister had
been a very close friend of hers.

We attended the funeral, of course, but I had made a mental
resolution to tune out the words of the burial service. I sat in the
pew, next to my wife, and concentrated my thoughts on a
business problem I had been wrestling with. Gradually, though,
the minister's words began to penetrate my consciousness. He
wasn't talking about the Lord God and Jesus Christ and the
promise of glorious everlasting life in the hereafter—he was
talking about our friend, about this woman, the sort of loving,
caring person she was, how she had lived, and how she would
be so sorely missed because of her influence and her nurturing
of her family and of all who came in contact with her throughout
her life. Now that minister had my full attention, and I was
moved, almost to tears, by his gentle remembrance of this dear
woman.

George Ikeson
Unitarian Fellowship
Houston, Texas

A person attending his or her first Unitarian Universalist funeral or
memorial service may be surprised. The focus is not upon the
deceased receiving a reward in heaven, and the intent is not to urge
the mourners to mend their ways and believe. The service, rather, is
about the person who has died, why he or she was special, what was
important in his or her life, why this person will be missed.

Friends may share memories and reflections upon the life of the
person who has died. Any one of those who have gathered may be
invited to share a thought. Sometimes the children or the spouse of
the person will speak. Sometimes, too, the minister will provide the
whole service, including his or her thoughts about the individual. But
in all cases the service will be personal—a response to one human
being's life.

The service also will recognize the loss experienced by those who
gather in this person's memory. Mourners seek support and reassurance that death does not erase life's meaning. The service is as much
for the people who gather as it is in memory of the deceased.

I remember the memorial service for my grandfather in the Unitarian church where he had been a member and in which I had been raised. It was the first memorial service I attended, and two things stood out for me. First, there was the support of the congregation and how the warmth of the people helped. The second thing was that during the service we in the congregation sometimes smiled, even laughed, as the minister shared memories of my grandfather. I was surprised because I had anticipated an occasion of unrelieved sadness. There was sadness, and there was loss, but there also was gratitude at having shared in this person's life. We felt enriched for having known him.

I remember people at whose memorial services I have officiated.

There was the woman born in Italy who came to New York at the age of nine. As an immigrant, she struggled to make her place in a new land. She married, raised three children and instilled in them her values of hard work, independence, education, making a contribution with one's life. When her husband died in 1937, she supported her family by working as a private pediatric nurse.

Work and family centered her life. She worked as a nurse until she was seventy-six years old. She was proud of being able to hold jobs and serve people even as she was getting old. She also was devoted to her family. She made many sacrifices to offer possibilities to her son and two daughters. When each grandchild came of age, she took him or her on a tour of Europe. In her later years, she thoroughly enjoyed the status of being the family's matriarch. She loved to be part of a celebration, any occasion in which she was surrounded by her family. At her memorial service, the family again gathered to mourn and to remember and express gratitude for the person that she had been. In the people whose lives she touched remained images of her values: family, work, independence, helping others.

I also remember a woman in her middle years who had lived courageously with cancer. "You know," she said to me the last time I saw her in the hospital, "I shouldn't be alive today." But she lived for many years beyond what had been predicted. She did not lie back and accept the prognosis: she questioned and fought it. In so doing she beat odds time and time again, and she rejoiced in each extra day she claimed.

She was a wonderful person to talk with: her spirit and courage shined through her conversation. She told me of her religious questioning, which led her into Unitarian Universalism. She told me about the things in our congregation she liked—and the things she didn't. She talked of her children—their entering adulthood and starting lives of their own. She talked of her second marriage and how important it was. She had received much support from her husband as they both lived with her cancer for the entire seventeen years of their marriage. As we gathered in her memory, her spirit and her independence still were with us. We felt grateful for having shared our lives with this woman.

Each of these people had touched others. Each was special. Each was mourned. We gathered to affirm their lives and in so doing to reassure ourselves. We gathered to affirm that life itself has worth.

❖ ❖ ❖

How can I live with death? By affirming life. By recognizing that life and death are interrelated—they are not separate.

A member of a congregation I served was stricken with cancer, and chose to live her final days at home. This was made possible by the support of members of the congregation. We supplied food and rides and company to back up the efforts of her family. As this woman lay dying, life was being renewed.

She said, "When I got sick, it brought people together." That was important to her. Another time she said, "I went to the symphony, and I was hugged and touched so much." And another time, "So many people help. I didn't know how many care."

She looked into life's mystery as death approached, and she found beauty: growing plants, flowers, cats, and the outdoors. She saw it in her children and in those she loved, and sometimes it was reflected in her smile. The last time I visited her, it was snowing. By now it was difficult for her to speak. She looked at the snow through the window and said, simply: "I love it."

A Unitarian Universalist minister wrote of his experience of life after having been diagnosed as having AIDS.

> As days went by, I regained some of my former energy. Early, I recognized that my future was not completely lost. I may have no future, I said to myself, but I have plenty of present. Each day is a gift—a sentiment which moved from platitude to deep truth with the words, "fatal illness."

In the midst of this I found I was loved far more than I ever believed. The outpouring of concern and support for me and my family was overwhelming. Our extended family—and the Unitarian Universalist movement, which is our tribe—rallied around in ways which astonish me still.

An ironic truth came home in the early weeks, as I found to my surprise how much love there was for me in the world. It was, after all, an act of love which unintentionally exposed me to the virus which has changed the framework of my life. Day after day, acts of love keep me alive. The friend who comes to Toronto from far away to see me; the meals, the gifts, the flowers, the many memories shared in conversation; such gifts of friendship reinforce my deep love of life, and remind me, above all, that it is love which gives us life and keeps us all alive.[3]

Humanity depends upon mortality. When I acknowledge that I am a limited being, life changes—existence assumes new meaning and mystery and beauty. With that recognition, we are transformed.

Notes

1. Richard Henry, "Norbert Capek—Unitarian Martyr," *The Church of the Larger Fellowship Bulletin,* June, 1982.

2. Donald Musser quoted by David C. Pohl in a letter to Unitarian Universalist ministers (April 17, 1988).

3. Mark DeWolfe, *The World* (July/August, 1989), p 36.

CHAPTER 8

What Brings Me Hope?

The question of hope directs us toward the future. What helps us face the new day?

Hope comes in different forms. Sometimes, hopes are specific—we hope for something, or for something to happen. I hope that I get into college—or out of college. I hope this person who is sick will recover. I hope I reach the goal I have set for myself. I hope something I fear won't occur.

Sometimes hope is that life will proceed in certain directions. I have friends who are involved in social causes that sometimes seem hopeless: peace, justice, equality. I wonder why they don't focus on more attainable ends. Once when visiting with such a friend, the answer came out. She said, "To be an activist is to take a long view. We know that what we advocate won't happen soon, but we just hope that what we do will nudge society a little in the directions we seek." And then she said, "That's why we don't get discouraged. We take the long view."

The hope of a Martin Luther King, Jr., or a Mohandas Gandhi was that of the long view. Certainly, they focused their activities on specific steps along the way, but the hope that drew them into the future could not be fully achieved—at least in their lifetimes: a fair society, a just society, a humane and compassionate society, a society in which people of different races and creeds could live together. It was a hope that guided their everyday activities and commitments, yet its realization was far in the future.

Sometimes, then, hope is specific—I know precisely the result I desire. And sometimes hope is general—hope is defined by principles, values, ideals. But at other times, I can't name a specific hope, and I can't identify a general value or ideal. Yet still I need hope. In times of trouble and stress, I seek an attitude of hope through which I am able to face the future. I need hope to approach the new day, even when there is nothing in particular I hope for.

Religion helps us conceive and articulate our hope. In orthodox Christianity, hope usually is expressed in terms of life after death when the faithful will be transformed to another level of being. In liberal Christianity, that transformation is more often expressed in terms of this world: the hope that this world may be transformed.

In Judaism, hope is gained from participating in a specific community with a shared history—a community chosen by God. In Eastern religious faiths, hope is conceived of as release from this world of suffering and pain. Rather than desiring eternal life, people of these faiths find their hope in getting off the eternal wheel of life.

We of the Unitarian Universalist tradition inherit an optimistic and hopeful faith. We view life as filled with possibilities. We take on challenges, fueled by a faith that human effort can meet challenges. We are encouraged to confront our personal concerns out of the hope that we can make our lives better.

The traditional Unitarian hope has been that by drawing upon human talents and capabilities, we can improve society and remake the world. Unitarians have found hope in the achievements of science and scholarship. We have promoted education, insisted upon better health care, fought for equal opportunity—all from the hope that these will help bring a better life. In the victories human beings have won over ignorance, disease, poverty and prejudice, we have found a hope that guides us into tomorrow.

The traditional Universalist hope has been expressed through the concept of a good and a loving God. Such a God, the Universalists believed, would not destine human beings to eternal punishment. Hence, the Universalist good news: there is no hell. In that image is an affirmation Unitarian Universalists have sought to apply to life in this world. We seek to bring people together in peace and understanding. We try to promote cooperation among those who differ. We try to show compassion for those who suffer. We resist the temptation to divide humanity into those who are "saved" and those who are "damned." For, as the Universalists have said, we all are children of a loving God. In that affirmation, there is hope.

The hopes articulated by the liberal religious tradition guide me, but they also fall short. Our efforts at improving society come apart; attempts to bring people together fail; human suffering continues, no matter what remedies we try; the world shows itself to be not as benevolent as we would wish. There are times when hope fails us— each of us becomes discouraged.

And so the challenge draws me forward. In this world that has such cause for despair, where can I find hope?

❖ ❖ ❖

Hope is revealed sometimes in unlikely situations. I found hope in a place that initially seemed to contain none at all: a state hospital where I worked as an orderly.

I will not forget the first time I walked in, my white orderly's uniform starched and fresh. The smell was the first impression; a mixture of disinfectant and urine. The look of the people was the next thing to hit. They surveyed me as I surveyed them, and they all seemed vacant, empty-eyed, not really human. And there was the background noise: a few words mixed with other bits of sound coming from people in pain or people who could not quite form words or people who didn't know that sounds were coming from their mouths.

This was a state hospital for people with incurable illnesses. The term "incurable" covered many categories. Some patients had terminal diseases. Others suffered from illnesses that were neither fatal nor curable. There were people with birth defects, the mentally ill, the senile, people who had suffered strokes or were victims of botched operations, people with alcohol or drug problems, some who had no place else to go. A few had been born at the hospital many years before when it had also served as a home for the poor and indigent. They had been raised at the hospital and never left.

The nurse gave me a tour and told me of the men on her ward. Many were moved from their beds to their chairs in the morning and then from their chairs to their beds in the evening. That's all they did. They stared at us as we walked by. One man, blind and deaf, was alone in a room because sometimes he became dangerous. He would flail his arms and yell, and he would cry. It was all very foreign to me until we came upon a scholarly-looking man who sat quietly, wearing dark-rimmed glasses and reading. Occasionally he looked up in disdain at some commotion going around; then he returned to his book. The nurse stopped, and we looked at him. She said, "He reads all day, but he never turns a page, and it's always the same book." The man didn't look up at her comment. He kept on reading whatever it was that he saw.

My first impression was that the hospital was filled with fragments of people, not human beings.

The other orderlies had ways of surviving. Some were cool and detached, never allowing themselves to get involved—a few were cruel—but many were able to draw human contact from the people they cared for and served. I learned as I watched these orderlies that people I considered vegetables became human when they were treated as human. They smiled and talked; their faces became animated. After the orderly moved on to give attention to another person, the expression in the person's face remained—for a while—before it sank again into the stupor characteristic of the ward. I was surprised to see the transformation in a person in response to human contact. It brought me hope.

Some patients talked with no one. Others were friends. There were those who struggled with each other, who fought for power and privilege; some were the butt of jokes. And I realized that this ward was a human community—a very complex human community. Its people had feelings and desires and worries and joys. Together, they created a society with its own rules and norms—its own culture.

One man would sometimes break into song. The song always was the same, "Take Me Out to the Ball Game." Usually the others ignored him. Sometimes they yelled at him to shut up. He wouldn't. But one afternoon others joined in—these men, old and young, together in their pajamas singing, "Take Me Out to the Ball Game."

It was funny—and a strangely joyous moment as well as an expression of community. Like it or not, these men were thrown together. They shared common turf; they spent their everyday lives with each other. In response to this predicament, they built a community—an unlikely community—but a human community.

In that I found hope. If human community can be formed under these conditions, then it can happen in many places. And if people in a state hospital ward can show a basic humanness, then I am encouraged to approach others with the hope of realizing common ties that join us all.

In this same state hospital lived a teenaged girl who spent her days in a wheelchair. She couldn't walk or talk; she opened her mouth and sounds came out, but they weren't words. She lived on a ward in which most of the other residents were old women. This girl, Karen, was a very lonely person.

My job was to visit people on that ward and talk with them. I was supposed to go up to each patient and have a little conversation. It sounded easy—it wasn't. It was hard work to go up and down a hospital ward and talk to people I didn't know.

It was especially hard with this girl, Karen, because when I talked with her she couldn't talk back. She opened her mouth, she made sounds, but they didn't fit into words. I didn't pause long when I came upon Karen in her wheelchair. I had been told that she couldn't understand what I said to her, anyway. So I would make a few remarks about the weather or the food at the hospital and then move on. I felt silly talking to someone who couldn't understand what I was saying.

One day I looked at her lips as Karen was making her grunting sounds, and it seemed that the sounds she was making were words. They meant something, and they were directed at me. My standard greeting when I went to a new patient was, "How are you today?" She was saying to me, "How . . . are . . . you?"

A few weeks later I was trying to talk and she was trying to respond. She was pointing at the tray that was propped on the arms of her wheelchair—almost like the top of a highchair for feeding babies. On this board were various designs, including an alphabet.

She had a hard time pointing because her hands were twisted, but I realized that she was pointing at letters one at a time and that the letters spelled words that she was not able to say herself. Another barrier was broken.

No, this was not a miracle. I pieced together the story that when Karen had entered the hospital, she could talk, and she was able to communicate through the use of the letter board. But this ward contained many patients, and nurses were stretched to their limits. Karen stopped trying to communicate; as new staff came onto the ward they assumed that she couldn't. I just happened to be the person who paid enough attention to get her to try again.

The memory gives me hope. When I find myself in a situation that seems impossible, I remember that occasion. I remember that human

contact can bring change. The memory helps me live with hope of
what yet may be.

❖ ❖ ❖

Sometimes, when life is not turning out as we would wish, it seems
that there is no hope. During times of pain and loss, when life is very
hard and few rewards come in our direction, we wonder: how can I
look to the future when the present seems so bleak? How can I find
hope amidst the hopelessness of these days?

A person has endured the death of a loved one, and then there
really isn't anything to hope for. There is only the challenge of
continuing to live.

A person has seen a dream come apart—perhaps the goals that
have given meaning to his or her life. Rarely can one dream simply be
substituted for another. For a while at least, we have to live without
a dream. That takes hope—not hope for anything that can be
named—just hope.

At such times I rediscover hope in emptiness, in darkness, in
silence. My wishes and ambitions are quieted, and I find a center to
existence that appears in emptiness, a light that becomes visible in
darkness, a sound that only I can hear in silence—an unobtrusive
noise in the background that I'm not aware of in the busyness of
everyday life. The sound of the refrigerator reminds me of this: it turns
off and only then do I realize that it has been chugging away in the
background. When it stops—in the silence—it seems that I can hear
life flowing through my veins.

Or, I wake up in the night from a frightening dream. I may not
remember what in the dream scared me, but I'm upset and need
reassurance. So, without wanting to wake anyone, I look at my family
asleep and listen for their breathing. I hear the breath of sleep, and I
am reassured. Life goes on.

Hope begins in quiet and in darkness and in times when the
confusion of the world is pushed aside so that I return to a central
truth: I share in a force of life that creates and sustains us.

When my marriage was falling apart, we were living in a
house in a wooded area, set back from the main road. There was
a dirt road that curved up the hill and the house on top. As you

drove up, there was a tree that grew on the rock outgrowth. It was a gnarled old tree, twisted by time, nourished by a thin covering of soil over bare rock. The years had exposed the roots which fiercely gripped the rock and help the tree in place.

As the months passed and I knew the marriage was beyond repair, the tree gave me strength to go on. I saw it living on and on, untended, little nourished, yet still surviving—and there were new leaves in spring, and even shade for passersby. It had survived and even produced beauty. It told me that I, too, would survive through the seasons and find my time of fulfillment.

Eleanor Milligan
Unitarian Fellowship
Frederick, Maryland

I talked with a social worker who is running a group for women going through separation or divorce. All of the ten, she said, came into the group saying that they most wanted friends with whom they could talk through what was going on in their lives. At the first session, they exchanged names and phone numbers.

A month—four sessions—later, the social worker asked, "How many of you have called one of the others in the group?" Not one. Why? "I was afraid of disturbing her." So: "How many of you would have been disturbed if called by another—any other—in this group?" No one. Each would have been delighted to *receive* a call.

It takes hope to break through the isolation; to say to another, "I need something but I don't even know what it is." It takes hope to offer your presence to another. It takes hope to put yourself at risk and enter the flow of life.

Hope comes from realizing that we share in a force of life that pulses through each of us. Even if our dreams come apart, even if our time on earth is limited, even if we face a period when there is little joy, still, there is hope where there is life.

❖ ❖ ❖

Life matters: this hope gets me through the times when I don't know what to hope for. It urges me to participate in life even when I don't know why—to make friends, plant trees, sing songs, bring children into the world. It is the hope that admonishes me to try to make a difference, that says it's worthwhile to share in another person's hopes and pain and to talk about my own. Everything depends upon the hope that life matters.

I found hope articulated at a meeting in which the speaker was a retired Unitarian Universalist minister. He had successfully served large congregations, published books, and was much loved and respected throughout our Unitarian Universalist community. He attended that meeting to share thoughts and responses to his recently published book.

But the memory I left this meeting with was not of my distinguished colleague as an author or as a minister. What stuck in my mind was a presentation he gave about the activity he had undertaken in retirement: tree farming. After he no longer served congregations, he moved to Maine and entered the life of one who plants and tends trees. I left that meeting with hope that came from his stories of raising trees.

I learned that tree farming is much like any other kind of farming. You promote the growth of the crop you want; you weed out the plants that compete; you fertilize, tend, prune, pray for rain. Even Unitarian Universalist ministers turn to prayer when the forest gets dry.

This is similar to kinds of farming I know about: corn farming, wheat farming, growing vegetables in the backyard. Except for one thing. He showed us a slide of a tree growing in his forest: a big tree that looked mature to my untrained eyes. He said, "This is what we're working toward—the tree is tall and straight, it's not crowded by other trees, but it doesn't take up too much space on its own either. When the time comes for it to be cut, this tree will be valuable."

"When," we asked, "will that be?"

"Oh," he replied, "in about fifty years."

Fifty years! I have a hard time waiting for tomatoes to ripen. But fifty years?

He showed us another picture. This featured very young trees just emerging from the forest floor. He said, "For these to grow, we have to clear away the less desirable trees, make space, provide light, insure moisture."

"When will these be ready for harvest?"

He replied, "You know, things happen slowly in Maine. I'd say they'll be ready in 80 or 100 years."

This man speaking to us probably was in his late seventies or early eighties. For him to be engrossed in an activity whose end he will never see is a statement of hope. It is a witness that life matters, even if we won't be around to see the results of our efforts.

What brings me hope? When I experience humanity in another person, when people overcome differences with respect for each other, when individuals come together to form a community: there is hope. When people show that they can change, when we affirm life even during those times which are hard, there is hope. Whenever people live with the faith that life does matter, then I find hope.

With that hope, I face the future. With that hope the present—even when difficult—can be affirmed and celebrated.

CHAPTER 9

Why a Liberal Religious Community?

T he affirmations of a religious tradition are expressed in its individual congregations. Since each tradition has different values and practices, congregations vary—each excels in certain areas. Each offers particular experiences and perspectives to its members, and each has a role to play in the larger religious community as well as the secular society.

I look to the congregations of other faiths for guidance as I pursue my own spiritual path. The Roman Catholic tradition offers a spirituality guided by a sense of creation's mystery and a liturgy that expresses that mystery. The Protestant tradition offers systematic theology and Biblical scholarship. Eastern religions provide an emphasis on faith as an ongoing quest rather than a static truth. Fundamentalists demonstrate fervor and commitment; Quakers offer social witness and an emphasis upon the inner light that resides within each of us. Judaism provides a tradition of scholarship and an emphasis upon family and celebration of life's holy days.

What are the contributions of the Unitarian Universalist tradition? What do we offer those who participate in one of our congregations, and what are our unique strengths within the larger religious community? Why do there need to be liberal religious congregations?

Daniel Walker Howe, a church historian and an Episcopalian, writes,

> One sometimes gets the impression that the Unitarian Universalist denomination today is an institution in quest of its own definition and purpose. There exist, however, both a

definition and a well-established role for the denomination that can be found in your history. What you will find there is a tradition of religious humanism.[1]

Despite the diversity among our members and congregations, we work from a common focus. Our starting point is the human condition, and our reason for being is to respond to the challenges of being human.

At a memorial service we remember and honor one person's life: what he or she valued, the good that this individual found in living. In a wedding service we stress the promises two people make to each other in creating their union. In our ceremony of dedication for children, we focus upon the commitments made to the children and to the parents as they take responsibility for the care of their child.

The same emphasis guides me in the ministry: I try to respond to the human condition—the issues and concerns with which we live each day. Responding to the human condition also is the aim of our involvement in social concerns issues. Generally, Unitarian Universalists don't get embroiled in abstract causes based on a vision of how things ought to be. Rather, we try to address the real sufferings and concerns and dangers involved in being human.

Many religions consider themselves God-centered or Bible-centered or tradition-centered. There is a place for that. But there also must be a corrective when God-centered or Bible-centered or tradition-centered religion becomes excessive and hurts people. For sometimes a commitment to God or religious authority or a vision of how life ought to be precludes the human. People are cast aside when they don't fit within the vision.

Many who have been hurt come to liberal religious congregations. When I hear people tell why they sought out a Unitarian Universalist community, I often am saddened by the harm that has been done by both secular and religious institutions. Not all of us experience it, but some people carry a deep and profound pain, and they come to us to be healed.

This is a story about the church as a saving community.

Shortly after I started grade school, my father abandoned my mother and me. When I was in third grade, we changed churches and began to attend the First Unitarian Church in

Providence, Rhode Island. I don't know if it was on my own initiative or at my mother's suggestion, but I went to the minister with my increasing hurt and disbelief over what had become of my world. He responded warmly and genuinely to this little girl who felt frightened and alone. He knew that I needed extra attention and he saw that I got it. There were seemingly always willing adults at the church to listen to me, to take me seriously, and to care for me. I am in earnest when I say that they saved my life.

Largely because of the trauma at home, I was a lonely child, hurt and angry. In public school I was often ridiculed for being too tall and gangly, and I was singled out because I had no father. At church school that never happened. I remember vividly my first day, the warmth of the teacher and the acceptance of me in the class by the other children. I don't remember the curriculum for that year, but I remember clearly how wonderful it felt to be in that class.

Martha Munson
Unitarian Universalist Church of Olinda
Ruthven, Ontario

I think of the variety of people we serve in Unitarian Universalist congregations. Some have asked too many questions in other religious institutions and have not been allowed to pursue their wonderings. There are people who have divorced and found they are no longer welcome in their religious home. Gays and lesbians come to our congregations seeking a place where they can affirm their whole being. Others come to us when they find that they can no longer accept the rules of their previous religious institutions in good conscience. Still others discover Unitarian Universalist congregations after finding that in too many other places their spirit—and their self—had to be denied in order to fit in. We offer a haven to those who are rejected in other communities.

Max Stackhouse, a United Church of Christ minister and professor writes,

I see a potentially great vocation for [the Unitarian Universalist] tradition: it can more self-consciously do what it often does accidentally. Namely, it can become the religious haven of those wounded by bad preaching, bad teaching, and bad pastoral care in more "traditional" communions.[2]

It's not accidental. The role of religious humanism throughout the ages has been to advocate religion and community that are human and humane, to protest when people are demeaned, to offer healing to those who have been hurt.

To return to the comments of Daniel Walker Howe,

Religious humanism has played an important historical role in the liberation of the human spirit from authoritarianism and obscurantism. It is a tradition that, in this country, has inspired some of the noblest efforts to fulfill the promise of American democracy.

One role that our congregations may play, then, is to represent the tradition of religious humanism, which advises us to take account of the human effect and sometimes the human toll of our practices and ideals.

❖ ❖ ❖

A congregation that affirms human worth and dignity must also be a congregation that values diversity. People enter Unitarian Universalism with a variety of backgrounds and life experiences. Thus we create religious community from a diverse membership. We also provide a place where differences may be bridged, and the walls that keep people apart may be lowered. One such opportunity presents itself at the interfaith marriages that Unitarian Universalist congregations often host. I remember the marriage of a Catholic man and Jewish woman in a Unitarian Universalist fellowship. The Catholics sat on one side, the Jews on the other. Between the two ran the aisle.

Everyone seemed tense and out of place. They hadn't been to a wedding like this before; they didn't know what was proper or how to behave. The groom was sweating and shaking. The only vow he and his bride had been able to agree upon was, "I do." He had trouble getting that out.

The end of the ceremony called for the Jewish tradition of the groom breaking a glass. This was a concession to the bride's side of the aisle. "You can do anything you want in your wedding," the bride's mother had said, "but I want the glass to be broken."

In these days of high technology, it sometimes isn't a glass that's broken. I hate to betray the illusion, but that object so carefully concealed in a cloth napkin is, in fact, a light bulb—it makes for a better pop when it breaks. But it would sound ridiculous to announce that now we'll break the light bulb so, instead, I say "Now the groom will break the glass."

I took the so-called glass, already wrapped in a white napkin, and gave it to the groom. He was still sweating and shaking, and I don't think he'd ever seen anyone do this. He put the glass on the floor, stomped on it, and it gave a mighty pop. For a moment he looked surprised. Then nervousness melted, and his expression changed, and he looked completely pleased with himself.

The Jewish side of the aisle broke into laughter and then applause; the Catholic side of the aisle joined in. The groom basked in the approval that was being expressed. The bride basked. A boundary had been broken along with the glass. A Catholic-Jewish, Jewish-Catholic congregation had been created. A marriage had begun.

Interfaith couples come to our congregations seeking not only a marriage ceremony that values both sides equally but also to find children's religious education that teaches the traditions of both parents. Interracial families also come seeking a common ground where all can be accepted. And families come who want to be part of a congregation that values and affirms differences, rather than being in a place where all are expected to be alike.

I feel privileged to serve such a congregation, and I have been enriched by the opportunity. From people of Jewish background, I have become acquainted with a tradition with both richness and power that has sustained its people during good times and bad. From Hindu and Buddhist members, I have learned about the worldview of Eastern cultures and how it sometimes can offer guidance out of the dilemmas into which Western culture has fallen. Black members have given me a view of how society looks different to black people than to whites. Gay and lesbian members have taught me that when a person's sexuality is denied he or she becomes less a person and must then struggle to reclaim self-respect. From women who have sought to be successful in a man's world, I have learned about barriers to equal opportunity. Unitarian Universalist Christians have helped me view the stories of Christianity from a fresh perspective. And from Unitarian Universalists who are religious liberals but political conservatives, I have learned that our own openness sometimes comes up short. I have learned to be aware of the hidden creeds we may conceal in an officially creedless congregation.

And so this is a function that Unitarian Universalist congregations play: to create religious communities in which diversity is affirmed, and to demonstrate to the larger society that people of different beliefs and cultures may live together with trust and understanding.

❖ ❖ ❖

In a diverse congregation, power must be shared and authority extended throughout the membership. Thus our congregations are guided by democratic principles.

Alice Blair Wesley and George Marshall have examined the history of the Pilgrim congregations that established colonies in Massachusetts.[3] They have shown that the Unitarian Universalist connection with the Pilgrims is more than institutional (the congregation established by the Pilgrims in 1620 is now a Unitarian Universalist church). We also inherit an ideal of non-creedal and democratic congregational organization.

The group that became the Pilgrims first gathered in England near the little town of Scrooby. They were religious dissenters who could not abide by the teachings and practices of the Church of England. Some were scholarly people who had studied the Bible and found in its words a spirit that was not expressed in the state church; others were tradespeople who cherished the freedom to guide their own lives and live by their own beliefs, still others were clergy who could no longer in conscience serve the church into which they had been ordained.

The organizing meeting, held in 1607, was described by one present. He wrote,

> There was first one stood up and made a covenant, and these two joined together, and so a third, and these became a church, say they.[4]

This congregation of diverse people came together by the simple act of making a commitment to each other. Its members did not pledge allegiance to external authority, they did not require assent to any doctrine or creed. Rather, these people made a promise that they would, together, create a religious community in which they would seek to live by the ways of the spirit as they perceived it.

Unitarian Universalist congregations also are bound together by a commitment we make to each other. Our promise is that we will together—without creedal requirement or submission to external authority—create a religious community. That simple promise contains many implications.

There is an interpretation of the nature and sources of religious authority. Religious authority, for us, is not vested in statements of doctrine, religious hierarchy, or sacred texts. Religious authority, rather, comes from within each individual who chooses to live as best he or she can by the truth he or she finds. Religious authority is centered in conscience and therefore is shared among the congregation. In the promise we make to create a congregation is an affirmation that we all have access to religious truth.

This promise to create a congregation has implications for ministry. In such a community ministry is shared: each person has the capacity and responsibility for ministry. Each can offer care and support to those who suffer, and each can seek truth and light.

This promise at the center of our tradition also prescribes a particular form of organization. We share authority, responsibility, ministry. In our congregations members have the opportunity to determine policies and set the directions of the church or fellowship. We are not ruled by a central authority but, rather, each individual participates in responsibility for the organization.

What we offer the wider religious community, then, is a democratic model of congregation. We offer the same ideal to the secular society. The Pilgrim communities in Massachusetts created democratic organizations that became models for the government of the new American republic. As James Luther Adams points out, this has been an important role of liberal religious groups.

What were originally elements of a doctrine of the church appeared now as ingredients of a political theory; the consent of the governed, the demands for the extension of universal suffrage, the rule of law over the executive and the principle of the loyal opposition. The conception of the democratic society is, then, a descendant of the conception of the free church.[5]

Adams also notes that the nations which have been vulnerable to authoritarian rule in this century—Germany, Russia, Italy—don't have strong histories of religious dissent. They lack the models and the experience of democratic organizations.

Democratic religious congregations are not easy to sustain, but the work necessary to do that has worth. For through it we offer an ideal of community in which people are joined together by a promise of mutual respect and a commitment to share responsibility. In such organizations we provide a laboratory for the democratic society.

❖ ❖ ❖

Another characteristic of liberal religious congregations is an insistence that the holy is greater than any of the forms that confine it.

We affirm that there is a religious dimension to all experience and regard efforts to capture the sacred into prescribed creeds, rituals or symbols as missing the wonder and challenge of existence. There is religious truth in the story of Jesus but also in the life of Buddha and of Albert Schweitzer. There is religious meaning in the Cross and the Star of David but also in a flower, a tree, and in a human face.

The sacred is present in the everyday, as Emerson declared,

> All things with which we deal preach to us. What is a farm but a mute gospel? The chaff and the wheat, weeds and plants, blight, rain, insects, sun—it is a sacred emblem from the first furrow of spring to the last stack which the snow of winter overtakes in the fields.[6]

I find the holy scattered throughout life, in ordinary and extraordinary times.

At a wedding far from any official religious structure—outdoors, in the backyard of friends who had supported this couple in good times and bad. Friends circled them as they made their vows, and in the background were sounds of birds and of wind blowing through the trees. In the feelings of the people present, there was something holy.

At a demonstration where I stood with others silently witnessing against policies of our government which we believed were wrong, receiving both taunts and encouragement from the passersby. As part of a movement to bring change, all of us that day touched the holy.

In a hospital operating room with artificial lights glaring and monitoring equipment bleeping—a most unnatural setting. Yet there my daughter was born, and each time I recall that occasion, I feel a flood of emotion that reminds me: here I experienced something holy.

On a morning after a snowstorm that brought New York City to a halt. As I walked, I experienced something I'd never before known in New York: the city was quiet. It seemed a cathedral draped in white which revealed a dimension of life always present, but usually drowned out by the noise of the everyday.

In a classroom with eight other people as we shared the stories of our religious journeys. From week to week, trust grew that brought us together and into each other's stories. In that coming together I found support, renewal, hope—I touched life's sacred dimension. In each of these moments, there is something of the holy. As Henry David Thoreau observed in *Walden,*

> In eternity there is indeed something true and sublime. But all these times and places and occasions are now and here. God himself culminates in the present moment, and will never be more divine in the lapse of all the ages. And we are enabled to apprehend at all what is sublime and noble only by the perpetual instilling and drenching of the reality that surrounds us.

Thus another of our roles within the wider religious community is to affirm an attitude of wonder and gratitude toward life. And to present alternatives when the holy becomes captive of a particular story or time or place.

❖ ❖ ❖

Unitarian Universalist congregations, then, have contributions to make to the larger secular and religious community. We offer congregations guided by the ideals of religious humanism in which there is acceptance of each other in the diversity of the human condition. Our congregations are democratically organized so that authority is shared, since each individual has access to truth. We also offer a perspective that affirms the many ways the sacred dimension of existence is experienced and expressed. We try to be open to the force of life that sustains and renews us.

People who participate in the liberal religious tradition find that our congregations offer particular kinds of experiences. One woman sees her church as a place of belonging and closeness that she has not found in other communities.

> Of all the world's round holes this square peg has ever tried to adjust to, the Unitarian Universalist Church is the only group I ever found that gives me feelings of belonging, safety, and acceptance. I need my church as a refuge.
>
> I need it as a substitute family for mine has never been close, nor has it offered the acceptance my church has.
>
> I need the human contact it gives me, for I tend to forget about others in my solitary pursuits. I need the opportunities it gives me to be a social person, to contribute to a group effort at making some higher effort succeed. I need the church because it gives me the chance to educate some liberals about how human the physically disabled are. I need to jar their conscious-ness for the disabled they come into contact with.
>
> I know the need is mutual, whether they know it or not.
>
> *Judy Lorincz*
> *Unitarian Universalist Church of Delaware County*
> *Media, Pennsylvania*

Another experiences her congregation as an environment of car-ing and support, even when she has made mistakes.

> As chair of the Sunday Program Center, I was introducing our keynote speaker of the year to a standing-room-only Sunday Service. Reading from a carefully prepared and practiced text, I concluded with, "...it is indeed a privilege to introduce to you our distinguished speaker from the Union Theological *Ceme-tery*."
>
> Well, the congregation burst into laughter, and I was about to burst into tears, when a dear friend jumped up from his

nearby seat and spontaneously gave me a big hug, and the laughter subsided into warm applause.

I have often thought of that moment, as I've ventured into a myriad of scary tasks and challenges in our Fellowship. I know now that if I make a mistake, I will be supported and loved no matter how terrible it seems and that only in taking risks and making mistakes, can life-enriching growth occur.

Lois-ann Sepez
Unitarian Universalist Fellowship
Huntington, New York

A woman who grew up in a black Protestant church in Brooklyn reflects about her move to a Unitarian Universalist fellowship and what she found there.

"A fellowship?" I thought to myself. It just sounded so different. Here I was, embracing a whole new religious community. My fears soon proved to be for naught. It was a group of loving, caring, and warm people who held common goals and values.

As I slowly became involved, I liked the way I felt about the fellowship. At first I was skeptical because it wasn't like any other church I had known. No thunderous church choir. No missionary group. No preacher shouting off the rooftop with religious dogma. Yes, I could be happy here.

This is because the people were just as wonderful as I had remembered from my past. They were everything one could hope for in a religious community.

I like being here. I feel at home. At last.

Helen Weeks
Unitarian Universalist Fellowship
Huntington, New York

Another woman reflects upon the generations of religious liberals who have participated in her church and of her hopes for the future of this congregation.

I am proud of our church and our religious ancestors who struggled to make our country the good that it is. I come to church to be with you knowing that some day others will be carrying on for us as we carry on for our religious ancestors. When I come to church I seek the wisdom to find how I fit into life and our lives. I look within myself to find myself and in looking within myself, I behold you who are also seeking. Together I hope we can find ourselves and in finding ourselves find the beauty of love, of life, of that which is eternal, God. This is what I want for our church always—to enlarge our circle of community as we grow together.

Nona Miller
Unitarian Church
Quincy, Illinois

And a Unitarian Universalist minister comments upon his understanding of the church he serves.

This church is not a place of right convictions, a fortress of truth or even a bastion of philosophy. The church is a community of those who have suffered loss, lived through it, and learned true compassion. They have a sense of awe and mystery about this world and this enterprise of living. Our church is where we hear music and sing it ourselves, where we serve one another, where the strands of our beliefs, our lives and hopes are WOVEN in a cable strong enough to bear us across the valleys of pain, despair, grief, doubt and disillusionment. Each has experienced these, or will. We learn from each other, and for those reasons we come to this special place, infusing it with hope.

Edward Harris
All Souls Unitarian Church
Indianapolis, Indiana

"You know," a new member of the congregation I serve said to me, "this is not the real world."

"Oh?" I said, without understanding. This person went on to explain.

It's not the real world because in the real world Christians and Jews and theists and humanists don't even try to live together.

And in the real world you don't seek to understand another person's ideas—you attack or ridicule or ignore them. In the real world gay people and lesbians and straight people don't share in the same life together. And in the real world people are kicked around a lot and nobody cares very much, and you can pray to your God to hurt somebody else, and that's acceptable.

And so you shouldn't think that this congregation is the real world because it isn't.

She may have been right: perhaps I don't know what the real world is, because I'm often surprised. I am surprised when religious people square off against each other with vehemence and fury; when individuals are used and then cast aside without even a word of regret; when the person who speaks truth is castigated and those who say simply what we want to hear are honored; when words of peace are used to promote violence, and words of liberty are used to promote the status quo, and words of justice are used to promote retribution. I am surprised when individuals are marked, labeled, categorized by race or religion or sex or sexual preference—and then when those who have done the labeling claim to know all there is to know about that other person.

I am *not* surprised when ideals we promote turn out to be beyond our reach, and we fail to live up to their promise—ideals are to make us stretch. I'm not surprised when real life falls short of what we want it to be.

But I am surprised when there is not even the attempt: when people seek no greater purposes than their own being, no greater meaning than whatever they happen across in a day, no greater understanding than what confirms their prejudices, no greater vision than the way things are.

I don't know if I should be pleased or appalled: appalled at the state of the world or pleased to be of a community that at least takes steps toward another vision. The point is to be aware that we of the liberal religious tradition try to live from a set of affirmations that are not shared by everyone. We have a faith that is not everyone's faith, and so we provide an alternative set of values, of being.

The liberal religious congregation may not be the real world, but we have something to offer that real world: an urging toward compassion, an encouragement to consider the human side of our problems and concerns, a reminder of the bonds shared by all people, an affirmation of freedom and tolerance and openness in our society.

This may not be the real world, but we are part of the real world, and we also live in tension with it. Why, then, should we create a liberal religious congregation? Through it we keep that tension alive and creative and productive, nudging this world a little in the direction of our dreams, as we offer each other our caring and support.

Notes

1. Daniel Walker Howe, "Through the Eyes of a Historian," from *The Unitarian Universalist Christian* (Winter, 1987), p. 26.

2. Max L. Stackhouse, "UUs: Wonderful! And Wrong?" from *The Unitarian Universalist Christian* (Winter, 1987), p. 49.

3. George N. Marshall, *The Church of the Pilgrim Fathers* (Boston: Beacon Press, 1950); Alice Blair Wesley, *Myths of Time and History,* 1987.

4. Wesley, p. 102.

5. James Luther Adams, *On Being Human Religiously* (Boston: Beacon Press, 1976), p. 9.

6. Quoted in W. C. Gannett, *Emerson: Selections from His Writings* (Boston: American Unitarian Association, 1925), p. 16.

CHAPTER 10

How We Would be Changed

I once had a conversation about marriage with a woman when we both were college students. We weren't talking about marriage to each other or to anybody in particular. This was an abstract conversation.

I said, "Different people bring out different parts of me, so the person I marry also will change the person I will be."

My friend disagreed. She said, "I'm always, essentially, the same. The person I marry won't change that."

Both of us were right in this argument. Of course, each of us remains the same person, so she was right. But I was right, too, for I respond in different ways to different people. I am changed by each person with whom I enter into relationship.

This phenomenon also happens in groups of people: different groups bring out different parts of ourselves. I respond differently in a group of Unitarian Universalist ministers than I do in an interfaith gathering. I'm different still with friends that I've known for a long time. In each situation different qualities are called for, different responses are appropriate. When I choose the groups to which I will be related, I choose who I will be.

Unitarian Universalist congregations are groups that change people. When we enter into relationship with a church or fellowship, some parts of ourselves are encouraged, others are not. Some beliefs are affirmed, and some are criticized or ignored. We are related to a particular view of the world, and in that process we are changed.

I have seen insensitive people become more caring through their experience in Unitarian Universalist congregations, and fearful

people become more confident. I have seen people who have been
hurt and angry become better able to accept life's possibilities and
limitations. Some have taken on challenges they would not earlier
have thought possible. Others have been moved to a wider vision of
the human community and their responsibilities to it.

In choosing to commit myself to Unitarian Universalist congregations, I too seek change. I hope to live with courage and affirmation
as I aspire to help others and make a contribution to the larger society.
To do that I need encouragement and support: I need to be changed
time and time again. What are the directions of change that can occur
in Unitarian Universalist congregations?

❖ ❖ ❖

I am changed as I seek to live the liberal religious affirmation of
respect for human worth and dignity. Robert Raible, addressing his
colleagues after fifty years as a Unitarian Universalist minister, observed,

> There is only one rule for being an effective minister in our
> free church. It is to be fond of people....
>
> Make no mistake about this. If you are entering our tradition
> because you like to preach, or because you know truths that the
> world ought to hear, or because you have ideals which you
> want others to practice, I beg of you to quit now, before it is too
> late, before you cause incalculable harm.
>
> You will be a useful minister only if you can love each person
> as a divine entity, as a child of God in human guise capable of
> infinite possibilities.

At the core of Unitarian Universalism must be respect for people. It
doesn't matter how brilliant or committed or talented we may be. If
we don't respect people, we indeed will do incalculable harm.

Respect for people means listening to another, giving our time and
attention to the person who shares his or her ideas and concerns. It
does not mean solving problems for others or telling them how we
think they ought to live or trying to save them from their troubles. It
does mean being with people as they struggle with the issues of their
lives.

Respecting human worth and dignity means acknowledging our connection with others, even people different from ourselves. It means recognizing that we of the human family are bound together, that our fate rests upon our learning to share the earth. Respect for people means affirming that each has something of the divine within, that each has something to contribute.

By trying to live with respect for people, I am changed. I am let into the lives of others—I see the world from their experience and perspectives. My view of life deepens and becomes more complete. I also am encouraged to work with people, inviting their involvement and considering their judgment. My decisions are more likely to be right, and projects more likely to work when they involve participation by a variety of people. My own vision is expanded as I respect the ideas and perceptions of others.

We are brought back to Channing's "view of the dignity of human nature which was ever after to uphold and cherish him." In trying to live that view I have been welcomed into the richness of other people's lives. I have benefited from their insights and been redeemed by their support. Because I have offered respect, people have shared themselves with me, and in that I have been changed.

❖ ❖ ❖

Unitarian Universalist congregations have encouraged me to respect myself and trust the validity of my own perceptions and convictions.

We often are told that there is much wrong with us. We receive that message from advertising, television, religion, from each other. But most people already are good at coming up with self-critiques; we really don't need others to add to the criticisms we already level at ourselves. What we do need—and what's much harder to get—is affirmation, support, a sense that we have worth and dignity. For it is only when we are accepted for who we are that we can risk growth and change.

From my first Sunday service, I was convinced that I had finally come home. I was welcomed warmly by the members and invited to the social events. I was extremely shy and introverted and had low self-esteem because of past life experiences in an authoritarian marriage and religion. When I was first asked to participate in a service, I was terrified but forced myself to cooperate as I know this was an egalitarian religion where every member's contribution was necessary and meaningful. Encouraging my first feeble efforts to say a few words in public, the fellowship gradually increased my self-confidence by their total, unswerving acceptance and support.

Gloria Bertonis
Lower Bucks Unitarian Universalist Fellowship
Fairless Hills, Pennsylvania

I think of people who have joined Unitarian Universalist congregations in the hope of finding support for themselves: a former fundamentalist minister trying to free himself from a faith he found to be repressive, a member of a charismatic group who came for support as she sought to take responsibility for her own life, a former nun who struggled to be born again in the secular world, a gay man who sought self-respect after a lifetime of denying who he was, the parents of a young man who had joined a separatist church and shut them out of his life. Each sought dignity, a sense of having worth, affirmation for who they were. Each sought change.

I too am best able to change in an atmosphere of acceptance. I have been in programs where the approach to change was to tear down a person before building him or her up again, in which sin and pride were perceived as the essential human problems that had to be overcome before progress could be made, in which following the rules or the experts or the leaders was given priority over developing one's own point of view. Some may benefit from such experiences, but I haven't. I have come into my own only when I have been helped to regard myself as a person of worth and dignity. Only then can I begin to trust my perceptions, my abilities, my dreams. Only then do I take the risk of investing myself in life.

❖ ❖ ❖

I also am changed through the Unitarian Universalist affirmation of the wonder and mystery of life. I am urged to regard life as a gift to be received with gratitude.

Among many Unitarian Universalists, especially those of long-standing, I find a characteristic outlook upon life: openness, anticipation, interest and involvement in the world. They have an attitude of experimentation, an ongoing wonder about the world and the human place in it. I remember talking with a Unitarian Universalist minister who had been retired for many years, and I was struck that our conversation did not revolve around what he had done and been in previous years. Rather, he said, "This happened to me last week, and I wonder what it meant." Or, "I shared this idea with people, and I was surprised at how they reacted." He continued to be engaged in life, and it occurred me that this attitude toward life—this willingness to be open and surprised—is part of the liberal religious message. In the everyday wear and tear of life, many people become disillusioned, expect the worst of people, become hardened in their attitudes and their opinions. Many approach their days with a siege mentality—"It's either them or me." Others become cynical or weary.

I know where it comes from. I am discouraged when life does not proceed in the directions I wish; I feel battered by waves of problems that just keep coming. On some days it's all I can do to keep trudging ahead in the hope that there are brighter times ahead. But that attitude has limitations: the mood gets harder to break, and life becomes too much trudging. I turn to the community of religious liberals where I am encouraged to affirm and embrace life, even when times are not what I want them to be.

The Unitarian Universalist minister Joseph Barth offers this observation in looking back over his long and successful career:

At this juncture in my life, I can state my faith with simplicity. This: I am faced each day with two miracles beyond understanding: the miracle of birth and of death. Between them I live in what is to me still largely a vivid mystery: life itself.

We reside in a context of mystery. Most of the time I don't experience it, but then something triggers my awareness—a small event, perhaps—and I am changed.

A child is dedicated before our congregation. We say words of shared responsibility, and a feeling of warmth extends through the people gathered. This feeling reminds us we are part of a larger community and a deeper force of life that is good and deserves to be celebrated.

At a memorial service where we gather to remember one who has touched our lives, friends speak, there builds a shared memory of the person and a sense of gratitude for having shared life with her. As we together affirm her life, we testify for the value of all life. As we acknowledge her worth, we find our own.

Sometimes it happens at a regular Sunday service. I may be speaking or it may be a lay service or perhaps during a musical selection. Three or four times a year this may happen: for an instant I feel an intense quiet—a quiet that goes deeper than the absence of noise. For moments I feel connected to everyone and to life itself.

Such occasions are fleeting, and normal consciousness again returns. But I remember them so that I may remain open to life's miracle and mystery—to embrace, to wonder, to be ever available for surprise. When I live with that awareness, I am changed.

❖ ❖ ❖

Through my involvement with Unitarian Universalist congregations, I also am urged to participate in life—to get off the sidelines and try to make a difference.

James Luther Adams writes,

> Human beings, individually and collectively, become human by making commitments, by making promises....The human being is the promise maker, the commitment maker.[1]

The argument between liberalism and orthodoxy goes on: do we have the right and the power to take responsibility for our lives and for our society? Can human action have any effect upon the world? The response of our tradition is to challenge us to use our energies and talents, to become involved.

It's an old message of our tradition, yet it still needs to be heard. For there are those today whose religious beliefs counsel them to accept life as they find it, to be content with their place, to refrain from challenging the status quo. And there are those of purely secular orientation who defend their resigned pessimism with the assertion that society is corrupt, always has been, and nothing we can do will change that. To counter such resignation, we need the liberal religious insistence upon engagement in the struggles of life.

My own natural inclination is to hold back from involvement. Yet, there's also a little Unitarian Universalist voice within—installed, I suspect, by a Sunday school teacher many years ago—that urges me to take the risk and be related to people in community. Because, the voice continues, this is what matters. This is what makes a difference.

This emphasis of our liberal religious tradition has changed me. It has changed our society. It continues to needle us when we become too comfortable. It is a challenge to religious orthodoxy, and it is a challenge to modern despair, and it is a challenge to everyday complacency: we can make a difference, we can be involved. In living the affirmation of involvement in life, we are changed.

❖ ❖ ❖

I began this book with questions, and questions have provided its focus. The answers I have worked out help me face the daily challenges and opportunities of my life, but I continue to wonder about these issues and to adjust my responses. Life *is* messy, and resists my attempts to arrange it in neat patterns. And so the challenge is to affirm existence while I am in the midst of its loose ends and ambiguities, to invest myself in life even when I don't have all the answers.

For underlying all is mystery. I don't know how wounds get healed and how people put aside difficult times and move on to better ones, but I know that they do. I don't know why, after talking through their problems, people become more relaxed—that their faces look happier and they stand straighter. I don't know how we absorb all the bad news of our days and still turn to the world with hope and affirmation, but I know it happens. I don't understand the mechanisms through which society is moved toward greater freedom, justice, and compassion, but I've seen it take place and know that such changes can occur.

I don't know how it happens: that's the mystery. But it feels to me that there is a force in the universe that gives us life, comforts and renews, inspires and grants us strength. It feels to me that the universe operates with a vital presence at its center.

Each person participates in this force of being. Each of us has something of the holy inside, and each of us has something of the holy to offer. I am, then, encouraged to seek that spark of the divine in myself, to nourish it in others, and to participate with joy and praise and gratitude as the drama of life unfolds.

The German mystic Meister Eckhart (1260-1328) observed, "If the only prayer you say in your whole life is 'thank you,' that would suffice." With the prayer of thanks I continue to pursue the questions of existence, guided and sustained as I am by the people of our Unitarian Universalist congregations.

Notes

1. James Luther Adams, *The Prophethood of All Believers* (Boston: Beacon Press, 1986), p. 137.

About the Author

Bruce T. Marshall has been minister of the Unitarian Universalist Fellowship of Huntington, New York, since 1981. He also served as minister of Unitarian Universalist congregations in Flint, Michigan and Decatur, Illinois.